GABRIEL
GARCÍA
MÁRQUEZ

A Study of the Short Fiction

Also available in Twayne's Studies in Short Fiction Series

Jorge Luis Borges: A Study of the Short Fiction by Naomi Lindstrom
Willa Cather: A Study of the Short Fiction by Loretta Wasserman
John Cheever: A Study of the Short Fiction by James O'Hara
Stephen Crane: A Study of the Short Fiction by Chester Wolford
Andre Dubus: A Study of the Short Fiction by Thomas E. Kennedy
F. Scott Fitzgerald: A Study of the Short Fiction by John Kuehl
John Gardner: A Study of the Short Fiction by Jeff Henderson
William Goyen: A Study of the Short Fiction by Reginald Gibbons
Ernest Hemingway: A Study of the Short Fiction by Joseph M. Flora
Henry James: A Study of the Short Fiction by Richard A. Hocks
Franz Kafka: A Study of the Short Fiction by Allen Thiher
Bernard Malamud: A Study of the Short Fiction by Robert Solotaroff
Katherine Mansfield: A Study of the Short Fiction by J. F. Kobler
Flannery O'Connor: A Study of the Short Fiction by Suzanne Morrow Paulson
Liam O'Flaherty: A Study of the Short Fiction by James M. Cahalan
Grace Paley: A Study of the Short Fiction by Neil D. Isaacs
J. D. Salinger: A Study of the Short Fiction by John Wenke
Irwin Shaw: A Study of the Short Fiction by James R. Giles
Isaac Bashevis Singer: A Study of the Short Fiction by Edward Alexander
John Steinbeck: A Study of the Short Fiction by R. S. Hughes
Peter Taylor: A Study of the Short Fiction by James Curry Robison
Tennessee Williams: A Study of the Short Fiction by Dennis Vannatta
William Carlos Williams: A Study of the Short Fiction by Robert Gish
Virginia Woolf: A Study of the Short Fiction by Dean Baldwin

Twayne's Studies in Short Fiction

Gordon Weaver, General Editor
Oklahoma State University

Gabriel García Márquez
Photograph courtesy of Wide World Photos

GABRIEL GARCÍA MÁRQUEZ

A Study of the Short Fiction

Harley D. Oberhelman
Texas Tech University

TWAYNE PUBLISHERS • BOSTON
A Division of G. K. Hall & Co.

Twayne's Studies in Short Fiction Series, No. 24

Copyright 1991 by G. K. Hall & Co.
All rights reserved.
Published by Twayne Publishers
A division of G. K. Hall & Co.
70 Lincoln Street
Boston, Massachusetts 02111

Copyediting supervised by Barbara Sutton.
Book design and production by Janet Z. Reynolds.
Typeset by Compset, Inc., Beverly, Massachusetts.

10 9 8 7 6 5 4 3 2 1

The paper used in this publication meets the minimum
requirements of American National Standard for Information
Sciences—Permanence of Paper for Printed Library
Materials, ANSI Z39.48-1984. ∞™

Printed and bound in the United States of America.

Library of Congress Cataloging-in-Publication Data

Gabriel García Márquez : a study of the short fiction / [compiled by]
    Harley D. Oberhelman.
        p.   cm.—(Twayne's studies in short fiction ; no. 24)
    Includes bibliographical references and index.
    ISBN 0-8057-8333-4
    1. García Márquez, Gabriel, 1928–   —Criticism and
interpretation. I. Oberhelman, Harley D. II. Series.
PQ8180.17.A73Z6735   1991
863—dc20   91-9679
                                                                CIP

Poets and beggars, musicians and prophets, soldiers and scoundrels, all we creatures of that disorderly reality have needed to ask little of the imagination, for the major challenge before us has been the want of conventional resources to make our life credible. This, my friends, is the nub of our solitude.

—*Gabriel García Márquez, Nobel Address, 1982*

Contents

Preface   xi
Acknowledgments   xiii

PART 1. THE SHORT FICTION

The First Short Stories and Journalism   3
Big Mama's Funeral: Social and Political Reality   19
Innocent Eréndira: Humor and Entertainment   36
Conclusion   53
Notes to Part 1   57

PART 2. THE WRITER

Introduction   63
Excerpts from *The Fragrance of Guava*   64
      Plinio Apuleyo Mendoza and Gabriel García Márquez
Interview, 1983   72
      Claudia Dreifus
Excerpts from *Seven Voices: Seven Latin American Writers
      Talk to Rita Guibert*   75
      Rita Guibert
"A Talk with Gabriel García Márquez"   78
      Marlise Simons
"Conversations with Gabriel García Márquez"   80
      Armando Durán

PART 3. THE CRITICS

Introduction   83
Raymond L. Williams   84
Regina Janes   89
Kathleen McNerney   98
Mark Millington   104

Contents

Chronology　　117
Selected Bibliography　　120
Index　　132

Preface

In 1982 Gabriel García Márquez received the Nobel Prize in literature, the just reward for more than three decades of dedication to the creative process in the short story, the novel, and journalism. Like many of his contemporaries in Latin America, he views his literary creation as a revolutionary process. He is a social critic in all of his fiction, and espouses a leftist ideological position. Nevertheless, García Márquez is not doctrinaire in his writing. He is able to capture the tone and meaning of Hispanic culture and tradition while at the same time communicating universal characteristics. He has always contended that the revolutionary role of the writer in the twentieth century is to write well.

This study focuses on the short fiction of García Márquez and its relationship to both his novels and his work in journalism. Various collections of his short stories have been published in Spanish and in English translation. In 1972 Harper & Row published his major short stories under the title *Collected Stories*. The volume contains 26 stories previously published in translation in three separate volumes. The great advantage of this collection is that the stories are placed in the chronological order of their original publication in Spanish. García Márquez's fiction clearly lends itself to a chronological analysis, for it is relatively easy to see in it a progression of both ideas and style from the tentative steps of the early short stories to the mature craft of the Nobel laureate. The three separate volumes brought together in *Collected Stories* correspond to three stages in the writer's career and are the basis of the three sections in the first part of this study.

This volume is the first in either Spanish or English to concern itself exclusively with the short fiction of the Colombian writer. It focuses on the evolvement of García Márquez's concern with solitude and death, with the irrational forces that control the lives of his protagonists, and with his dubious estimation of science and technology. The society he describes is one beset by the jolting effects of civil strife and exploitation. His characters struggle to comprehend the role in life that fate has decided they must play.

Preface

I am deeply indebted to many colleagues and friends in the United States and Colombia who have contributed in great measure to the realization of this project; to the College of Arts and Sciences of Texas Tech University for generous research grants, and to the university for two faculty development leaves that enabled me to pursue my research on García Márquez. I also wish to recognize my obligation to the librarians and curators of the following universities, institutions, and newspaper archives: the Luis Angel Arango Library and the Caro y Cuervo Institute, Bogotá; *El Espectador* and *El Tiempo*, Bogotá; *El Universal* and the Bartolomé Calvo Library, Cartagena; *El Heraldo*, Barranquilla; the Hispanic Division of the Library of Congress; the Alderman Library of the University of Virginia; and the Texas Tech University Library.

Acknowledgments

I am grateful to the individuals and publishers listed below for granting permission to reproduce the critical studies in parts 2 and 3 of this volume. Special mention is made of the permission granted to quote from *The Collected Stories of Gabriel García Márquez*, © 1984 by Gabriel García Márquez, reprinted by permission of Harper & Row, Publishers, Inc.

Plinio Apuleyo Mendoza and Gabriel García Márquez, excerpts from *The Fragrance of Guava*, translated by Ann Wright, reprinted by permission of Verso Editions. Rita Guibert, *Seven Voices: Seven Latin American Writers Talk to Rita Guibert*, excerpts reprinted by permission of the author. Excerpts from "The *Playboy* Interview: Gabriel García Márquez" by Claudia Dreifus, *Playboy*, February 1983; © 1982 by *Playboy*, reprinted with permission, all rights reserved. Marlise Simons, "A Talk with Gabriel García Márquez," excerpts from the *New York Times Book Review*, 5 December 1982; © 1982 by the New York Times Company. Armando Durán, "Conversations with Gabriel García Márquez," excerpted from *Review 70* 3 (1971), published by the Center for Inter-American Relations. Excerpts from *Gabriel García Márquez* by Raymond L. Williams, © 1984 G. K. Hall & Co., reprinted by permission of Twayne Publishers, a division of G. K. Hall & Co. Regina Janes, excerpts from *Gabriel García Márquez: A Study of the Short Fiction*, by permission of the University of Missouri Press, © 1981 by the Curators of the University of Missouri. Kathleen McNerney, excerpts from *Understanding Gabriel García Márquez*, © 1989 University of South Carolina Press. Excerpts from *Gabriel García Márquez: New Readings*, edited by Bernard McGuirk and Richard Cardwell, © 1987 by Cambridge University Press, reprinted with the permission of Cambridge University Press and the author, Mark Millington.

Part 1

THE SHORT FICTION

The First Short Stories
and Journalism

Four months after the May 1967 publication of *One Hundred Years of Solitude*, Gabriel García Márquez, in a conversation with the Peruvian novelist Mario Vargas Llosa, asserted that good literature always shows a tendency to destroy that which is established, that which is imposed, and to contribute to the creation of new societies and the betterment of life for humanity. In the same dialogue he repeated his frequently quoted statement that the principal political duty of a writer is to write well.[1] Later, in an extensive interview with Plinio Apuleyo Mendoza, García Márquez avowed that in general a writer writes only one book, although that book may appear in several volumes under different titles.[2] Often one of the volumes stands out far above the rest, so that the writer seems to be the author of one primordial work.

The extraordinary success of *One Hundred Years of Solitude*, and of at least two subsequent novels, proves his point. Following the critical success of *One Hundred Years of Solitude* throughout the world, critics began to evaluate his earlier short stories, novels, and newspaper articles. Collections of short stories and novels published after 1967, such as *The Autumn of the Patriarch* and *Love in the Time of Cholera*, have also become best-sellers and won wide critical acclaim. In 1982 he was awarded the Nobel Prize in literature, a high measure of recognition for the first of 16 children of a telegraph operator from the dusty village of Aracataca on the Colombian littoral.[3]

A close reading of his early endeavors provides an overview of his emerging style and shows the broad vision of the mythical world behind all his narratives. These early writings contain the themes and methods that recur throughout his fiction. Moreover, he emphasized in his Nobel acceptance speech, he starts from the reality of everyday events in Latin American life, events so surreal that he does not have to invent hyperbole.[4] He writes about simple people in the remote, isolated reaches of Colombia, imbuing them with a literary soul in much the same way William Faulkner dealt with the inhabitants of his Yoknapatawpha County.

García Márquez spent little time with his parents during his childhood years. His parents' marriage was not favored by the bride's family, and the couple left Aracataca shortly thereafter to live in various coastal cities. Their first child, Gabriel José, was born on 6 March 1927. For the first eight years of his life he was left to the care of his maternal grandparents as his parents moved about in an effort to better their economic situation. García Márquez's grandparents undertook his education in the local Montessori school and later sent him to the Jesuit secondary school, Colegio de San José, in Barranquilla. School records show he attended this institution from 1940 to 1942, that he was an alert and competent student, and that he contributed original prose and verse to the school journal, *Juventud*. Receiving a scholarship to the Colegio Nacional in Zipaquirá, García Márquez made the arduous journey there by boat up the Magdalena River and then by train to the high plateau to complete his secondary education. For one who had spent his entire young life on the tropical coast, the journey brought a dramatic change in climate and life-style.

Bogotá was a different world, populated by somber masses carrying black umbrellas to protect themselves from the cold rain. The secondary school nearby was located in an unheated convent, and the young Gabriel was forced to find in books an escape from the dismal reality around him. Among his favorite volumes were *The Magic Mountain*, *The Three Musketeers*, *The Hunchback of Notre Dame*, *The Count of Montecristo*, and the works of a band of young Colombian poets who had formed a coterie called Piedra y Cielo (Stone and Sky) (Mendoza, 39–45). He completed his secondary school diploma on 12 December 1946 and, after a brief visit with his parents, entered the law school of the National University in Bogotá in 1947.

The course of Colombia's history and everything in García Márquez's personal life changed dramatically on 9 April 1948 when the charismatic leader of the Liberal party and candidate for the presidency, Jorge Eliécer Gaitán, was assassinated in downtown Bogotá. His death unleashed a vengeful furor among the masses and plunged Colombia into a violent period of chaos, subsequently called *la violencia* (period of violence) by historians, that spread like a raging fire to nearly every corner of the republic except the Caribbean coast. Its effects were to last some 14 years, and the scars of conflict between Liberals and Conservatives are still visible today.

García Márquez's career as a writer began only a few months before the violent cataclysm unleashed by Gaitán's death. His first three short stories had appeared in the "Fin de semana" ["Weekend"] section of *El Espectador* in late 1947 and early 1948, but the ensuing riots caused the boardinghouse in which he was living to burn, thereby destroying some of his unpublished manuscripts. The National University where he was studying law was immediately closed, and García Márquez left Bogotá for Cartagena, where the political strife was negligible and where he could continue his study of law. Cartagena also offered the possibility of a continued association with journalism in the newly established daily *El Universal*. During the nearly two years he lived in the coastal city, García Márquez contributed 38 articles, most of them in a column called "Punto y aparte" ("Period, New Paragraph"), and he continued to produce short fiction.

The First Short Stories, 1947–1955

As noted, García Márquez was a contributor to *Juventud* while still a secondary school student in Barranquilla; however, the short story "The Third Resignation," which appeared in the "Fin de semana" section of *El Espectador* on 13 September 1947, is generally considered his first publication. Prompted by a statement by Eduardo Zalamea Borda of the *El Espectador* staff that the new generation had nothing to offer the literary scene, García Márquez wrote "The Third Resignation" as a rebuff and was amazed to find it published within the week. There was nothing to do but continue to write, and "Eva está dentro de su gato" ("Eva Is Inside Her Cat") appeared on 25 October 1947, followed by "Tubal-Caín forja una estrella" (Tubal-Caín forges a star) on 17 January 1948.

The principal theme in most of his early short stories is death, and "The Third Resignation" pulsates with an agonizing fear of this inevitable reality. His reading of Kafka is clearly visible in this first short story. He recounts that when he read *Metamorphosis* at the age of 17, he realized he could be a writer (Mendoza, 30). The transformation of Gregor Samsa into a gigantic beetle was a revelation to García Márquez of the exciting other literary possibilities outside the rational examples he found in his secondary school texts. His first short story seeks to emulate Kafka's defiance of everyday reality and to fuse the fantastic with the routine.

"The Third Resignation" relates the death of a child of seven from typhoid. The family doctor is able to prolong the boy's life even beyond death: "[h]e was in his coffin, ready to be buried, and yet he wasn't dead."[5] The text moves to a more objective level as the narrator views the child's death retrospectively. But the reader is suddenly returned to the Kafkaesque world of a "second" death when, at the age of 25, the protagonist ceases to grow in his coffin. Now the body begins to decompose and give off a foul smell. The protagonist realizes he is to be buried "alive," that he faces "life" from the depths of the grave. Perhaps he will return to the biblical dust of death and later "rise up the capillary vessels of an apple tree and awaken" (*CS*, 10). It will be like living again, but by then he will probably be so resigned to his condition that he "might well die of resignation" (*CS*, 12).

An omniscient narrator, so close to the protagonist that the story at times seems to be a monologue by the deceased, takes the reader through the successive stages of a universal human experience. As the effort of a beginning writer this tale contains a surprising degree of thematic unity. The central idea, an attempt to bury a corpse, will appear later in his first novel, *Leaf Storm;* in the short story "Los funerales de la Mamá Grande" ("Big Mama's Funeral"); and in the novel *The Autumn of the Patriarch.* The central idea of multiple death is often seen in his later fiction. There is a coherence in this story's point of view, but its dense vocabulary often leads to complex and tortuous syntax. For a first short story, however, it clearly reveals the technical control and universal thematic concerns that characterize his later fiction.

In "Eva Is Inside Her Cat," one of the longest of his early stories, again the topic is death and reincarnation. Eva suffers the curse of beauty as she wanders about through a kind of spiritual limbo. She is in a world of darkness, but at the same time she longs for a return to "real" life and decides to seek a free existence in the body of her cat. Momentarily she fears that she may prefer mice to her favorite human foods, but then discovers a great concern—the cat is nowhere to be found. Not only is the cat missing, but her house is no longer the same. Everything is different; a pervasive smell of arsenic fills the air. Only then does she understand that 3000 years have passed since she first dwelled in the world of the living.

Like the protagonist of "The Third Resignation," Eva is "alive" for the 3000 years since her death. Both stories explore the fantastic and deal with inexplicable events. Two and a half months later *El Espec-*

tador published "Tubal-Caín forja una estrella." Mario Vargas Llosa calls this effort a story diffuse to the point of incoherence.[6] It has appeared neither in any of the several volumes of García Márquez's collected short stories nor in English translation. Raymond L. Williams characterizes it as "a classic piece of youthful experimentation with language" and calls it "one of the weakest stories of those written in this period."[7] The Kafkaesque motif of mice is present again during a nightmare of memories that race through the mind of a suicide moments before the rope closes around his neck. Here again the story is related from the point of view of someone already dead (or in the process of dying), and the confused rush of memories produces a hallucinatory interior monologue.

"La otra costilla de la muerte" ("The Other Side of Death") and "Diálogo del espejo" ("Dialogue with the Mirror") are in essence the same story. First published in 1948 and 1949, respectively, both were written during the period García Márquez was studying law in Bogotá, but both appeared in *El Espectador* after his departure for Cartagena. "The Other Side of Death" introduces the idea of a double, in this case an identical twin who is dead. The protagonist fears that the spatial limits separating the two are merely illusory, that they both share a common identity. Insomnia terrorizes the surviving brother, and a series of disquieting dreams aggravates his restless imagination. In the end he resigns himself to death, the only thing that stands between him and his deceased brother.

This was the first short story of García Márquez published in Bogotá after his departure, and he probably left it behind in the newspaper office when he left the capital. Some six months later "Dialogue with the Mirror" appeared for the first time, also in *El Espectador*. A footnote on page 11 of the 23 January 1949 edition in which it was published indicates that it is related to "The Other Side of Death," and is, in fact, a continuation of the same story. Here the same protagonist awakens, gets out of bed, stands before the bathroom mirror, and starts to shave. What he sees in the mirror is the reflection of his dead twin brother, who perfectly imitates his every move. Suddenly the face in the mirror begins to bleed, but the protagonist can find no cut on his own face: "[T]here in the mirror, a face just like his contemplated him with large, stupid eyes and the face was crossed by a crimson thread. He opened his eyes and smiled (it smiled). Nothing mattered to him anymore" (*CS*, 46).

These short stories all explore the same world of inner reality. Ambiguity hovers over them, and the stylistic pitfalls of youthful inexperience are clearly evident. Robert L. Sims characterizes the short stories of this first phase as dominated by omniscience, lack of character development, Kafkaesque morbidity, and descriptive abstraction.[8] Although "Amargura para tres sonámbulos" ("Bitterness for Three Sleepwalkers") is from the same period (13 November 1949), it marks the first occasion of William Faulkner's influence in García Márquez's writing.[9] Its date coincides with the year that Faulkner's "A Rose for Emily" first appeared in Spanish translation in the Cartagena press.

"Bitterness for Three Sleepwalkers" signals a shift from the internal to the external and from the abstract to the concrete. It is about a girl who fell from the second story of a house, becoming permanently disabled and crippled. The tale is narrated in the first person plural by three insomniac brothers. A great deal of time has passed since the accident, and the girl lives in a hallucinatory world in disarray: "Once she told us that she had seen the cricket inside the mirror glass, sunken, submerged in the solid transparency, and that it had crossed through the glass surface to reach her. We really didn't know what she was trying to tell us" (*CS*, 38). Such wild affirmations do not seem to surprise the three, who resign themselves to her ultimate death: "we knew that she was sufficiently human to go along willing the elimination of her vital functions and that spontaneously she would go about ending herself, sense by sense, until one day we would find her leaning against the wall, as if she had fallen asleep for the first time in her life" (*CS*, 39). The language of this short story is considerably more direct than that of its predecessors.

Two stories that follow chronologically also use the first person: "Ojos de perro azul" ("Eyes of a Blue Dog") and "Alguien desordena estas rosas" ("Someone Has Been Disarranging These Roses"). The former was used as the title of the first authorized collection of the early short stories of García Márquez,[10] but the story itself is a less-than-satisfactory example of his early prose. Mario Vargas Llosa calls it "the most poorly executed, the most confusingly structured of all the early stories" (Vargas Llosa 1973, 457). All of the action takes place in a world of dreams, as a woman attempts to track down in real life a presumed lover from her dream world. In the dream the phrase that is the story's title is the name the lover gives her as a kind of secret code between them. Unfortunately, he never remembers any of this when he is awake. The reader is left confused and frustrated by the enigmatic and ambiguous nature of the plot.

"Someone Has Been Disarranging These Roses" is much more successful. The narrator is a dead boy—reminiscent of the narrator of the first short story, "The Third Resignation"—who opens with the surprising observation that "[s]ince it's Sunday and it's stopped raining, I think I'll take a bouquet of roses to my grave" (*CS*, 78). The narrator has, in fact, been dead for 40 years. He has "lived" in a single room for most of that time, and for the preceding 20 years a woman he knew as a childhood playmate has been sharing the house with him, unaware of his presence as she goes about selling flowers. Each Sunday the boy tries without success to take a bouquet of roses to his grave. His efforts leave the flowers in disarray, apparently scattered by the wind, the woman thinks. The boy's spirit dreads the day when the woman will die, for then he will be alone forever in the room.

This short story, written in 1952, marks a higher level of technique than many of its predecessors. The idea of a specific town in which the action takes place is a preview of the immanent invention of Macondo, the fictional town celebrated in his best-known novels and short stories. Vargas Llosa appropriately observes that "the amorphous reality of the early tales is beginning to take on a recognizable shape. It has begun to move within fixed limits, the same limits that will govern its development, its growth and regrowth in future years" (Vargas Llosa 1973, 459). The first sentence in the story requires the reader to suspend his disbelief and accept the possibility of action—at least on a mental level—after death. Once this is accomplished, the story moves forward within the bounds of this new reality. Here García Márquez has successfully employed the techniques of "magical realism" that characterize his most ingenious later fiction.

"La mujer que llegaba a las seis" ("The Woman Who Came at Six O'Clock") represents García Márquez's first attempt at police fiction. He insists that it resulted from the loss of a bet he made with his long-time friend Alfonso Fuenmayor that he would not be able to write such a tale. The author himself calls it the worst love story he could possibly write.[11] Among its many faults, García Márquez points out, are that the dialogues are stilted and that it is an obvious imitation of Hemingway. "La noche de los alcaravanes" ("The Night of the Curlews") is a combination of realism and the grotesque. García Márquez uses the collective first-person-plural "we" to narrate the story of three men who have been blinded by an attack of curlews.[12] The story is presented almost entirely in dialogue.

He told Plinio Apuleyo Mendoza that in his opinion there is a wide gulf between spoken and written Spanish dialogue, and he uses dialogue scantily in most of his writings (Mendoza, 33). Like so much of the fiction of this period in García Márquez's life, "The Night of the Curlews" has an open, unresolved ending. A feeling of solitude and abandonment prevails. The anonymous human voices around the blind men are unable or unwilling to come to their aid; some even believe that their story was a fake item made up by the newspapers to boost circulation. In the end the three blind men are totally disoriented: "We sat down. An invisible sun began to warm us on the shoulders. But not even the presence of the sun interested us. We felt it there, everywhere, having already lost the notion of distance, time, direction" (*CS*, 88). Curlews here make their first appearance in García Márquez's canon; later they will become an important motif in *Leaf Storm* and *One Hundred Years of Solitude*.

From Cartagena, and later from Barranquilla, García Márquez continued to send occasional short stories to *El Espectador*. His reputation as a writer and journalist continued to grow, but Cartagena became an increasingly limited area for his expanding literary interests. In early 1949 García Márquez left to visit his parents in Sucre (today called Sincelejo), taking the only route available: by boat, which required a trip first to Barranquilla. At the time Barranquilla seemed a much larger and more stimulating environment for the young intellectual, and by the end of the year García Márquez decided to return to the city where he had begun his secondary education to work as a columnist for *El Heraldo*.[13]

The cultural milieu in Barranquilla at that time was dominated by the Catalonian poet and dramatist Ramón Vinyes and by the Colombian novelist José Félix Fuenmayor. Together they were the heart and soul of the Grupo de Barranquilla (the Barranquilla Group), which included young intellectuals who were to become García Márquez's closest friends. A variety of other writers and painters joined the group from time to time. The association of García Márquez with Vinyes and the Grupo de Barranquilla was crucial to his later writing, as well as to his interest in the work of William Faulkner. The presence of Faulkner in the short stories published after his arrival in Barranquilla is readily apparent.

"Nabo: The Black Man Who Made the Angels Wait"

With the publication of "Nabo, el negro que hizo esperar a los ángeles" in 1951 García Márquez's prose achieves a more definitive representation of the theme of solitude that permeates his later writings. It is here that the idea of solitude comes into its own as an inescapable factor of human experience, one that limits an individual's ability to experience a full measure of life.

In "Nabo" García Márquez creates a character with a name (something rarely seen in his earlier fiction) and explores social problems through that character's story and milieu. The setting is in a region similar to the Old South of the United States, a place where black servants attend aristocratic ladies on plantations. An omniscient narrator and a first-person-plural "we" alternate in telling the story of Nabo, a young black boy who grooms horses on the plantation and plays the gramophone to entertain an idiot girl. The name Nabo means "turnip," the only word the girl is ever able to speak.

On Saturday nights Nabo would go to the town square to watch a black man play the saxophone. But the black man stops coming to the square and disappears from his life. One morning a horse kicks Nabo in the forehead, leaving his mind in turmoil for the rest of his life. His masters have him bound hand and foot and lock him in a room where food is regularly passed to him. This tragic state continues for 15 years until in a fit of rage "the huge bestial Negro . . . came stumbling over the furniture, his fists raised and menacing, still with the rope they had tied him fifteen years before" (*CS*, 76). The girl, now a grown woman, sees him pass by and utters the only word she ever learned, "Nabo."

There is yet another level of narration—an interior one—closely related to the external action just outlined. Nabo lives in a timeless ebb and flow for 15 years after the accident, recalling Benjy's sense of time in Faulkner's *The Sound and the Fury*. Faulkner's presence, in fact, is most perceptible in the temporal fragmentation of the action and the multiple points of view of the narrators. Nabo's only vivid memory is of the horse's hoof shattering his forehead. Then one day he hears a voice calling him; it is the black saxophone player urging him to join him in a celestial choir: "We're waiting for you, Nabo. There's no longer any way to measure the time you've been asleep" (*CS*, 73). Nabo hesitates; he remembers the horses he once tended and the special comb he used to groom their tails. The saxophone player urges

Nabo to act: "[i]f the only thing you're waiting for to come to the choir is to find the comb, go look for it" (*CS*, 76). At this point Nabo breaks down the door and escapes past the idiot girl, who utters his name. The two levels of narration—external and internal—are thereby perfectly joined.

Donald McGrady's 1972 study of "Nabo" was the first to point out the Faulknerian techniques used in this and others among García Márquez's early short stories.[14] "Nabo" is closely related to the ideas of Faulkner's *The Sound and the Fury*. Both employ multiple points of view and chronologically move from a point in time near the end of the action backward and forward without any discernible temporal pattern; only at the end do they fit together into a unified narrative. Nabo in this story is in charge of an idiot girl; two of Faulkner's black boys, Versh and later Luster, have identical roles in relation to the idiot Benjy, the narrator of the perplexing first section of *The Sound and the Fury*. Both Benjy and Nabo have a similarly acute sense of smell. But perhaps the highest degree of similarity between the two works is the dignity both writers give their black protagonists. The blacks of *The Sound and the Fury* hold the Compson family together through trial and tribulation; in the words of Faulkner, they "endure." The abandonment of Nabo stands in stark contrast to his care and attention for the idiot girl during their childhood. She remembers almost nothing, but she does remember the one person who once cared for her and taught her to crank the gramophone. Nabo's heartless masters are incapable of understanding, much less explaining, the relationship between him and the girl, but her gratitude is expressed when she calls out his name as he stumbles out of his prison.

"Nabo" also continues the techniques and themes first seen some two years earlier in "Bitterness for Three Sleepwalkers." Both deal with disabled or feebleminded girls, and multiple first-person-plural narrators relate both stories. By the time "Nabo" appeared, García Márquez had achieved the ability to use language skillfully and to give his story structural symmetry and coherent unity. The abject solitude of Nabo and the idiot girl is a link to García Márquez's first novel, *Leaf Storm*, and to his later fiction.

"Monologue of Isabel Watching It Rain in Macondo"

When asked whether it is true that every writer spends his life writing a single book, García Márquez answered in the affirmative, declaring that his single book was the "book of solitude" (Mendoza, 59). In the short story "Monólogo de Isabel viendo llover en Macondo" (1955) he names his creation for the first time, calling it Macondo, a place lost in an ambience of abject solitude.

Jacques Gilard has established the publication of a slightly different version of this text in *El Heraldo* on 24 December 1952, with the title "El invierno" ("Winter").[15] This was, in fact, García Márquez's last publication in the Barranquilla daily. The text was reissued in 1955 in *Mito* with 11 relatively minor changes from the 1952 version. The earlier version was accompanied by a note suggesting that it was a chapter of the as-yet-unpublished *Leaf Storm*, and it does indeed seem to have been written originally as a part of the novel, though it does not appear in the printed edition of it. As noted by Frank Dauster, the story is a portrait of a woman whose severe depression is exacerbated by the oppressive, crushing force of a five-day tropical downpour.[16] This phenomenon will recur in García Márquez's later fiction and will be a central incident in *One Hundred Years of Solitude*.

The genesis of this short story and of the entire Macondo canon has been described by García Márquez in several interviews. In his 1983 *Playboy* interview he describes the gestation of the concept of Macondo, declaring that it began to take shape when he was about 21 and accompanied his mother on a return visit to Aracataca to sell the family home.[17] To his surprise, Aracataca seemed suspended in time; "I realized that all the short stories I had written to that point [ca. 1950] were simply intellectual elaboration, nothing to do with my reality. I immediately sat down and wrote my first novel which takes place in Macondo. Incidentally, on that trip my mother and I passed a banana plantation I had often seen as a child. There was a sign on the place; it was called Macondo" (Dreifus, 172).

In 1967 "Monologue" had been published in Argentina, together with a study of García Márquez's short stories, in the form of a small book of 46 pages called *Isabel viendo llover en Macondo*. In this work Macondo is a clearly defined hamlet and not the vague, abstract setting of his earlier short stories. In addition to Isabel, her husband, Martín, is also present, as are her father (the colonel of *Leaf Storm*) and her stepmother. The diluvial episode begins with the words "[w]inter fell one Sunday when people were coming out of church. Saturday night had been suffocating. . . . Then it rained, and the sky was a gray, jellyish substance that flapped its wings a hand away from our heads" (*CS*, 89). At first the rain is refreshing, but as time passes a feeling of boredom prevails. Isabel remembers the heat of August when their clothes stuck to their bodies; suddenly an overwhelming sadness crushes her soul: "At sundown on Tuesday the water tightened and hurt, like a shroud over the heart. . . . We no longer saw anything except the outline of the trees in the mist, with a sad and desolate sunset" (*CS*, 92). Everyone lost track of meals; the somber spectacle produced a terrible feeling of emptiness in Isabel, and a sour and penetrating smell of death permeated the atmosphere. "Monologue" ends with the villagers confused as to time, lost in the somnambulism of uncountable hours. Isabel believes she is dead. The sky has cleared, but all around Macondo there is a mysterious silence, and an invisible person seems to be smiling in the darkness. In the mix-up of time Isabel believes they are calling her for last Sunday's mass.

"Monologue" represents a clear line of demarcation between the early short stories and the later fiction of Macondo and beyond. García Márquez continues to explore the themes of time and space, but "Monologue" is more inventive and more successful in its examination of solitude. Raymond L. Williams offers a valuable key to understanding this short story in the following terms:

> The use of a first-person narrator is key to the creation of the sense of disintegration that pervades the story. The natural limitations of a narrator within the story who is also the protagonist create the instabilities that are key elements of the story. The basic narrative situation is that a first-person narrator tells the story in retrospective fashion, referring to the events exclusively in the past tense. . . . García Márquez employs a first-person plural ("nosotros") when the narrator refers to the immediate situation—the weather—and a first-person singular ("yo") when the narrator evokes the past. . . . The perspective of the story, like the substance of the fictional world, is in flux. Ideology and narrative point of view thus are joined in this experience of disintegration. (Williams, 26)

García Márquez skillfully combines the deterioration of the physical surroundings (Macondo) with the progressive change in the mental state of Isabel and other family members. It is possible in this story to perceive the writer's growth as a narrator as he shapes ordinary events into the extraordinary and the surreal: "[t]hen there was no Thursday. What should have been Thursday was a physical, jellylike thing that could have been parted with the hands in order to look into Friday. There were no men or women there" (*CS*, 95). The enigmatic suggestion at the end that Isabel is dead should not be viewed with surprise in light of similar circumstances in such earlier short stories as "The Third Resignation," "Eva Is Inside Her Cat," and "Someone Has Been Disarranging These Roses." The added element of suspense highlights the evolution of the writer's skill over a five-year period from the tentative beginnings of the first short story, published in 1947, to the relative mastery of both theme and technique in "Monologue."

As Williams fittingly demonstrates, this story also marks another giant step forward, the fictionalization of the reader (Williams, 27, 150). The awareness of the reader of fiction and the ability to manipulate this fictionalized entity will constantly unfold as García Márquez matures as a writer. The publication of "Monologue" in final form in 1955 coincides with the publication of García Márquez's first novel. The invention of Macondo has been realized, but the evolution of this fictionalized interpretation of Aracataca will continue for more than a decade.

Other Short Fiction and Journalism

The relationship between journalism and literature has always fascinated García Márquez. The reality that he learned to extract from his experience as a journalist is the stuff in which his fiction is steeped. Robert N. Pierce believes that all the themes of his later fiction, as well as many of his writing techniques, can be found in the news stories, articles, commentaries, columns, and reviews he produced for newspapers before he became well known as a writer of fiction (Pierce, 64). His careers in both fiction and journalism developed almost simultaneously during the early years from 1947 to 1955, and indeed it is difficult, if not impossible, to separate the two genres during this period. Contrary to Jacques Gilard's assertion that, despite its high quality, García Márquez's journalism would not be of interest today were he not renowned as a creator of fiction (Gilard, 32), it is clear that from journalism he learned the value of establishing high reader interest in the very first lines of a text (the "lead"), and of seeking original expository techniques. Moreover, García Márquez asserts that by read-ing good literature he learned to be a good journalist.[18] Such a sym-biotic relationship is the hallmark not only of his early writing but also of his work even today.

García Márquez's contributions to the Cartagena and Barranquilla press (1948–52) and his first writings in the Bogotá press after his return to the capital in 1954 have been collected and studied by Gilard in the first volume of *Obra periodística,* called *Textos costeños* (Coastal texts). Williams calls 10 of these pieces "Marquesa" fiction, for they deal with an imaginary marquesa and her husband, Boris, whose adventures seem to take place in India (Williams, 150). These early pieces, all published during the first half of 1950, evoked positive reader response from the Barranquilla public. Of somewhat greater interest is a series published in December 1952, called the "La Sierpe" series. McGrady calls these seven vignettes an introduction to a world not unlike Ma-condo (McGrady, 150). A sense of the marvelous and the prodigious informs the series, and the reader is required to suspend belief in ac-cepted reality in a manner akin to that of magical realism. Another set of fictional pieces appeared during the same period as "Apuntes para una novela" (Notes for a novel), and they are even closer to the fiction of Macondo than the "La Sierpe" series. These notes include charac-ters with the same names as the protagonists of *Leaf Storm* and *One Hundred Years of Solitude.* Additionally, six other "notes" experiment with techniques and topics later found in Macondo fiction.

Early in 1954 García Márquez's close friend, the poet and critic Al-varo Mutis, invited him to return to Bogotá to do motion picture re-views and editorials for *El Espectador.* The six years spent in Cartagena and Barranquilla had been artistically productive. He took with him to Bogotá the draft of a novel he has never published that bore the ten-tative title "La casa" (The house). He left behind in Barranquilla a coterie of close friends, the celebrated literary Grupo de Barranquilla. In Bogotá he worked from February 1954 until July 1955, at which time *El Espectador* sent him to Europe as a correspondent.

The Story of a Shipwrecked Sailor

Quite by accident, one of the most memorable stories García Márquez wrote after returning to Bogotá was a series of 14 installments in *El Espectador,* later published as a small book with the title *Relato de un náufrago* (1955; *The Story of a Shipwrecked Sailor*). It is the story of a

Colombian sailor, Luis Alejandro Velasco, one of eight crewmen on the destroyer *Caldas* who had fallen overboard and disappeared during a storm in the Caribbean in 1955. The ship was traveling from Mobile, Alabama, where it had been repaired, to Cartagena, where it arrived two hours after the tragedy. Ten days later Velasco washed up half-dead on the coast after having drifted on a raft without food or water. He was later given a hero's welcome in Bogotá, but after 20 six-hour interviews with García Márquez it came out that the cause of the accident was not a storm at all, but rather the shifting of boxes of luxury contraband articles on the deck of the ship. This revelation enraged the navy, as well as the government of the dictator, Gustavo Rojas Pinilla.

Although not strictly a work of fiction, *The Story of a Shipwrecked Sailor* is a first-person narrative fictionalized by García Márquez. In it he describes experiences Velasco had in Mobile, including episodes with a girlfriend with the improbable name of Mary Address and adventures at a favorite bar, Joe Palooka's. After the accident, tension builds during the 10 days Velasco is adrift on the makeshift raft. Sharks are an ever-present menace, and Velasco periodically suffers hallucinations and bouts of depression caused by the profound solitude of his condition. The experiences encountered by the sailor remind the reader of similar episodes already noted in the discussion of García Márquez's early short stories. The chronicle may belong to Velasco, but the language is that of the author of *Leaf Storm*.

Originally the 14 installments were proffered as entertaining journalism with no hint of historical purpose or political intent, but when García Márquez published them in book form in 1970, he added a prologue that left no doubt about his polemical intent. He stated that "the account, like the destroyer, was loaded with ill-secured moral and political cargo."[19] Velasco refused to recant even a word of his story, and the Rojas Pinilla dictatorship countered with a series of drastic reprisals that months later resulted in the shutdown of *El Espectador*.

García Márquez, in the meantime, had begun a nomadic exile in Paris, drifting, like Velasco, on the raft of financial insecurity. When *El Espectador* was closed, the wandering journalist in Paris was without a salary to support himself. Two years later, however, the Rojas Pinilla dictatorship collapsed, and Colombia was at the "mercy of other regimes that were better dressed but not much more just" (*Sailor,* ix). There is a disquieting postlude to this story; after the newspaper installments ended, Velasco dropped from public view while the government tried to discredit him. Some months later a reporter discovered him by chance working behind the desk of a Bogotá bus station. He looked as if life had passed him by, but the aura of a hero who had told the truth persisted.

By the mid-1950s García Márquez had established his reputation. Although he said he would destroy some of his early short stories if he could get his hands on them, they have been rescued from oblivion in the files of the newspapers that first published them.[20] They indicate the emerging mythical world behind his fiction, and illustrate his emerging style. Written as they were during a period of great national upheaval, they show how he reacted to the violence and censorship of the time. Above all else they affirm his dedication to aesthetic principles and to the precept of writing well.

Big Mama's Funeral:
Social and Political Reality

Some of García Márquez's best short stories are in the 1962 collection published under the title *Big Mama's Funeral*. His first novels–*Leaf Storm, El coronel no tiene quien le escriba* (*No One Writes to the Colonel*), and *La mala hora* (*In Evil Hour*)—together with the short stories of *Big Mama's Funeral* are the true antecedents of *One Hundred Years of Solitude*. The second and third novels were written during the difficult years in Europe, and most of the short stories were written during the period he spent there and later in Caracas, where he worked for the newspaper *El Momento*.

As the level of violence grew in Colombia in the decade after the assassination of Jorge Eliécer Gaitán in 1948, García Márquez's level of political consciousness began to identify him more closely with the national drama as he observed it first from Europe and subsequently from Venezuela. Although the second and third novels are not set in Macondo, three of the short stories in *Big Mama's Funeral* do continue the development of this fictional creation. The two novels and several of the short stories take place in an unnamed town referred to as *el pueblo* (the town), probably modeled on the river port of Sucre, where his parents lived for a time after leaving Aracataca. The creation of a new milieu for these novels corresponds to an effort on the part of García Márquez to free himself from the Faulknerian tag the critics so often pinned on *Leaf Storm*.

In any case, most of the short stories in the *Big Mama* collection concentrate on the vicissitudes of life in the closed environment of a small Colombian town, irrespective of whether it is called Macondo or simply *el pueblo*. *Big Mama's Funeral* is a transitional work between the early short stories and his mature fiction, yet the influence of Faulkner is always evident. It is not so much his style or use of multiple narrators as it is the reappearing characters, family clans, and recurring episodes that show the continuing influence of Faulkner's method. These short stories represent a sophisticated form of expression of the social and political realities of Colombian life as distantly viewed by the writer from his vantage point in Europe and Venezuela. He deals with the problems of human dignity and the plight of the poor, as well as with the political violence during the decade after Gaitán's assassination. Other themes seen in this collection are the problem of class differences in Colombia and the role of the artist in society. Throughout this volume the struggle of the humble to maintain their personal dignity as they face the power of the hierarchy above them is constantly in evidence. An element of humor, previously absent, is apparent, especially in the title story. These stories were written during the five-year period between 1955 and 1960, but none was published until 1962, when all eight appeared in a single volume published by the university press in Jalapa, Mexico.

"Tuesday Siesta"

"La siesta del martes" ("Tuesday Siesta") relates the visit of a woman and her daughter to a small, dusty town during the intense heat of a Tuesday afternoon. They have arrived by train for the express purpose of visiting the town's cemetery, where a week earlier the woman's son had been buried after being shot during a robbery attempt. The mother and her daughter have come to place a bouquet of flowers on his tomb. The heart of the story is an interview between the proud mother and the village priest, who controls the keys to the cemetery. Also present during the interview are her daughter and the priest's sister, who serves as his housekeeper.

In his conversation with Plinio Apuleyo Mendoza, García Márquez reveals that he considers "Tuesday Siesta" his best short story (Mendoza, 48). He recognizes the "purely technical tricks" he had learned from Hemingway and put to work in this masterpiece. The choice of Tuesday for the action of the story is no doubt based on the well-known Spanish proverb "*martes, ni te cases ni te embarques, ni de tu familia te apartes*" (Tuesday, don't get married or take a trip, or leave your family). The central idea, the dignity and pride of a poor woman in the face of ecclesiastical authority, recalls the theme seen earlier in *Leaf Storm*. García Márquez insists that the idea for this story is based on an incident he remembers from his childhood in Aracataca. One day a woman and a girl came to town, and the rumor spread that the woman was the mother of a thief. Her dignity and strength of character profoundly impressed the young García Márquez (Harss and Dohmann, 328).

The tone of this short story is objective and impersonal, providing sufficient details but carefully eliminating anything excessive or unnecessary. It opens with a description of the train trip: "[t]he train emerged from the quivering tunnel of sandy rocks, began to cross the symmetrical, interminable banana plantations, and the air became humid and they couldn't feel the sea breeze any more" (*CS*, 99). The heaviness of the oppressive heat stands in contrast to the dignified pride of the woman as she approaches the "enemy" town: "[t]here was no one at the station. On the other side of the street, on the sidewalk shaded by the almond trees, only the pool hall was open. The town was floating in the heat" (*CS*, 101).

As the two approach the parish house, they come face to face with the metal grating on the door that bars their way: "'I need the priest,' she said. 'He's sleeping now.' 'It's an emergency,' the woman insisted" (*CS*, 102). When the priest finally appears, he suggests they wait until sundown. But the woman is firm and determined; the return train leaves at three-thirty. After she states her son's name and explains that he was killed in the town the previous week, the entire incident is related in detail to the reader. This recapitulation is valuable, for it connects this short story to people and incidents that will appear in later works. The putative thief was shot by the lonely widow, Rebecca, who used an ancient revolver not fired since the days of Colonel Aureliano Buendía. Both Rebecca and Aureliano Buendía are major characters in *One Hundred Years of Solitude* and appear briefly in other novels and short stories. The mention that Rebecca has spent "twenty-eight years of loneliness" focuses the reader's attention on the central theme of many of the stories in this collection.

The conclusion is effectively stated in dramatic fashion. The priest and his sister, aware that groups of curious people have filled the streets, realize that the woman and her daughter will have to face a hostile crowd on their way to the cemetery. "Wait until the sun goes down," says the priest; "[w]ait and I'll lend you a parasol," adds his sister. "Thank you . . . we're all right this way," the woman replies in a proud, confident voice (*CS*, 106). She takes the girl by the hand, and they go out into the street.

Dignity and pride cause the woman to refuse the parasol. The visit to the town puts the social and economic disparity between the mother-daughter and the priest-sister into sharp relief. To the priest's question of why the mother did not ever get her son on the right track, she replies, "He was a very good man. . . . I told him never to steal anything that anyone needed to eat, and he minded me" (*CS*, 105). The priest could only offer the rejoinder "God's will is inscrutable" (*CS*, 105). In the end the mother, sure of herself and of the propriety of her actions, boldly faces the ominous challenge of a hot Tuesday afternoon in the streets of an unfriendly town.

"One of These Days"

Whereas "Tuesday Siesta" is related to other García Márquez writings through the use of reappearing characters and themes, "Un día de estos" ("One of These Days") describes an incident that occurs in greater detail in the novel *In Evil Hour.* The incident, however, is presented from different perspectives in the two works. In both instances the mayor of a nameless town has endured days of pain due to an abscessed wisdom tooth, and his visit to the local dentist is an unwilling act, since they belong to bitterly opposed political parties. In neither version does the reader know which party either supports, but in both works the mayor is an oppressive military figure.

The short story focuses the action on the dentist, Don Aurelio Escovar, whose 11-year-old son announces the arrival of the mayor to have a tooth pulled. "Tell him I'm not here," replies the dentist; "[h]e says if you don't take out his tooth, he'll shoot you," responds the son (*CS*, 108). The effects of war and violence are at once seen in the natural, matter-of-fact reaction of the son to the mayor's threat. Because of the abscess, the dentist must extract the tooth without anesthesia, saying "[w]ithout rancor, rather with a bitter tenderness, . . . 'Now you'll pay for our twenty dead men'" (*CS*, 109).

Kathleen McNerney correctly points out that in this short story "war and civil repression are skillfully understated, or unstated" and that violence has become a part of the status quo.[21] The use of understatement is one of the technical stratagems García Márquez learned from his early reading of Hemingway. The portrayal of the dentist is sympathetic; he is fearless and dedicated to a profession that he practices with meticulous attention. The mayor's use of threat and violence offers a stark contrast. Their confrontation takes place in a town where the effects of violence are evident in the crumbling ceiling and dusty web with spider's eggs and dead insects that decorate the dentist's office, and in the two pensive buzzards perched on the house next door to the office. The town has fallen into social erosion and economic stagnation, with no resolution in sight. When the dentist asks if he should send the bill to the mayor or to the town, the reply, "It's the same damn thing," reveals the morass of pessimism and futility into which this society and its political processes have fallen (*CS*, 110). The dentist's vengeance, extracting the tooth without anesthesia, will not ameliorate the violent circumstances that surround the town and its inhabitants. Frustration with social and political conditions will persist long after the mayor's toothache has vanished.

"There Are No Thieves in This Town"

The longest story in this collection, "En este pueblo no hay ladrones" ("There Are No Thieves in This Town"), deals with the theft of three billiard balls from a small town's pool hall, an act that deprives the inhabitants of their major form of recreation and hopelessly complicates the life of Dámaso, the thief, and of his 37-year-old wife, Ana, who is 16 years older than her husband. The whole community talks incessantly about the theft, but none will admit there are thieves in their town. Roque, the owner of the pool hall, falsely states that 200 pesos were also taken in the robbery. Dámaso and Ana are faced with the problem of what to do with the billiard balls, while wild rumors, most of them totally false, circulate throughout the neighborhood. A black man who happens to pass through the town is accused of the crime and thrown into jail. Since Dámaso cannot sell the balls, he decides the best thing to do is return them. He is caught in the act, and Roque demands the 200 pesos as well, "not so much for being a thief as for being a fool" (*CS*, 137).

The fact that Dámaso will no doubt suffer greatly because of his actions relates the central event of this story to many examples in literature of disproportionate punishment for relatively minor crimes. At the same time the story highlights the dull, backwater existence the inhabitants of such a small town lead. The theft becomes the talk of the town and produces an abundance of gossip and idle speculation. The disparate versions of the event Ana and Dámaso hear far exceed reality and reach a point where they almost convince themselves the townspeople's version is factual. In this respect the story is related to the events in the novel *In Evil Hour,* wherein the mysterious appearance of anonymous lampoons on a town's walls lead to bitter conflicts and unresolved tensions.

Character development is an important innovation of this short story. Because of its length, it is possible for the author to paint a detailed picture of the shiftless Dámaso, who drifts aimlessly from one activity to another, engaging in futile daydreaming and the invention of impractical schemes to get rich. Ana, older and more practical, concerns herself with the task of making ends meet and with the possible fate of the black man unjustly jailed for Dámaso's theft. George R. Mc-Murray concludes that the plot of this short story "is based on a well-conceived idea for the revelation of human weakness and the ironies resulting therefrom."[22] Its excessive length and inclusion of unrelated episodes, however, make it one of the less successful in the collection. It recalls some of García Márquez's early experimental efforts and at the same time reminds the reader that Hemingway's style is still clearly evident.

"Balthazar's Marvelous Afternoon"

In the form of an allegory, "La prodigiosa tarde de Baltazar" ("Balthazar's Marvelous Afternoon") addresses the role of the artist in society and the contentious problem of class differences. Except for the title story, this tale has received the greatest amount of critical attention of any in the collection, and is frequently included in anthologies. The story lends itself to a variety of traditional critical approaches, to structuralist and Marxist explications, and to reader-response theories. It clearly focuses attention on the creation of a fictionalized reader, and García Márquez carefully builds what Williams calls "a relationship of confidence between the author and the reader by assigning the reader a privileged position in the text" (Williams, 48). Together with the next short story in the collection, "La viuda de Montiel" ("Montiel's Widow"), the author creates an integral unit that serves as a transitional point between his earlier writing and his subsequent texts. The collection's title story completes the transition and sets the stage for *One Hundred Years of Solitude* and more recent short stories and novels.

Susan Mott Linker reduces the two tales to the constituent units of a myth in the following terms:

A simple, visionary man [Balthazar] makes a marvellous object [a prodigious bird cage]. A well-to-do neighbor [Dr. Octavio Giraldo] tries to buy the object, but it has been made for, and is destined to the son of a rich and repressive miser [Mr. Chepe Montiel]. The miserly father angrily refuses the gift, because he considers it an attack on his authority and position. The simple man leaves the gift with the furious miser, and celebrates his moral victory with friends and neighbors, who make of him a hero, and his victory their own. The miser eventually dies of a fit of anger, and his lands and business deteriorate and fail. His wife dies abandoned, and his children are scattered to other parts of the world.[23]

Linker reduces the central theme of these two tales to a treatise on the collapse of an old and established economic order under the challenge of new social and philosophical systems (Linker, 89).

Throughout "Balthazar's Marvelous Afternoon" García Márquez posits a series of opposites: Montiel/Balthazar; rich/poor; egoism/generosity; buying/giving; diffidence/confidence; unhappiness/happiness. Balthazar, in his role as artist, creates a thing of beauty at the request of the spoiled Montiel child. Ursula, his practical wife, urges him to ask 60 pesos for it, double what he had planned to ask. Dr. Giraldo attempts to buy the cage, but Balthazar insists it was made for the 12-year-old boy. The 60-peso price convinces the doctor not to buy, and he concludes, "Montiel is very rich" (*CS*, 142). Subsequently Montiel refuses even to consider buying it, for he had not been consulted when the deal was made. By this time the cage has become, in the mind of its creator, a work of art beyond the realm of monetary value. His noble gesture, giving the cage to the undisciplined boy, allows Balthazar to win a moral victory over the rich man, whose house he had approached with the "decorous candor with which the poor approach the houses of the wealthy" (*CS*, 142). Montiel unceremoniously sends him away with the retort, "The last thing we need is for some nobody to give orders in my house" (*CS*, 145). This last statement marks a clear delineation between the two social classes in the town.

When Montiel arrives at the pool hall after the presumed sale, he receives an ovation from his friends, who think he has extracted 60 pesos from the man who represents wealth and power. Balthazar treats everybody to a round of drinks (for which he has to leave his watch in pawn), and then, like Dámaso in "There Are No Thieves in This Town," engages in a fabulous daydream in which he makes and sells a thousand and then a million cages. "We have to make a lot of things to sell to the rich before they die," he says; "[a]ll of them are sick, and they're going to die" (*CS*, 145).

At this juncture García Márquez introduces the outline of class struggle between a capitalist, interested in the accumulation of wealth, and an artist of the proletariat, who attempts to rescue his art from the marketplace, where it would become another mere commodity. This act leads Beth Miller to conclude that the art object in this story acquires a symbolic value in the struggle between rich and poor.[24] The role of the artist in third-world societies is a corollary to Balthazar's actions. His friends leave him delirious with happiness in "a lighted room where there were little tables, each with four chairs, and an outdoor dance floor" (*CS*, 145–46).

This phrase is an obvious reference to Hemingway's short story "A Clean, Well-Lighted Place," which also speaks of individual integrity in an empty, alienated world. Miller suggests that in the García Márquez story the artist Balthazar can find salvation through moral, ethical, or political action (Miller, 57). The "sick" wealthy class, here represented by Montiel, can be overcome by artistic excellence, in this case the prodigious cage generously given to all who saw and enjoyed it. It follows, then, that a "poor" third-world novelist can sell his books and not sacrifice his artistic integrity.

Name symbolism is another important aspect of "Balthazar's Marvelous Afternoon." Balthazar's name can easily be related to that of one of the three Magi who sought the Christ child and brought gifts that included, among other things, myrrh, an aromatic, bitter embalming resin (Miller, 90–97). Montiel (*monte-hiel*, "mountain of bitterness") suggests the idea of Christ's sacrifice at Golgotha. Balthazar is counseled by his wife, Ursula, regarding the price he should ask for the cage. Her name is derived from the constellation Ursa Major ("great bear"), related in turn to the polestar, a guide for many a traveler. This name will later be used for the matriarch of *One Hundred Years of Solitude*. Dr. Octavio Giraldo's first name is related to the Roman emperor Octavian, likewise mentioned in the story of the Magi.

Such use of name symbolism points to a myth present in this story and suggests as a logical inference that "the eternal rebirth of Balthazar's challenge must inexorably lead to the decline and destruction of Montiel and his repressive system" (Miller, 97). That Balthazar is a kind of Christ figure is likewise confirmed by the biblical name Belteshazzar, also used as a name for the prophet Daniel. In the García

Márquez story, Balthazar, like Daniel, refuses to worship the gods of silver and gold (Dan. 5:23). Montiel, like the Babylonian king in the Book of Daniel, is doomed to die and his empire to disintegrate (Dan. 5:30). Balthazar's age (about 30), his physical appearance, and his trade as a carpenter also enhance his Christ-like image. He is abandoned, as was Christ, by his friends; his shoes are stolen; and women on their way to early mass avoid him because they believe he is dead.

"Montiel's Widow"

Balthazar's challenge to Montiel seems to be for naught at the end of "Balthazar's Marvelous Afternoon." He is abandoned in a drunken stupor in the street; he is in debt from the previous night's libations and has no money to retrieve his pawned watch. Some six or more years have passed when the action of "La viuda de Montiel" ("Montiel's Widow") begins, and it opens with the statement "When José Montiel died, everyone felt avenged except his widow; but it took several hours for everyone to believe that he had indeed died" (*CS*, 147). Most surprisingly, he died of natural causes and was not the victim of revenge. The rest of the story paints a picture of the town's most hated individual and of the subsequent deterioration of his land and fortune once they pass into the hands of his oblivious widow, who "had never been in direct contact with reality" and who takes no interest in the family estate (*CS*, 148). While Balthazar does not appear in this story, he is a part of the vengeful populace that boycotts Montiel's business and steals his cattle.

Before his death Montiel was a master at political chicanery. Working in league with the new mayor, Montiel began his career as a confidential informer. Together he and the mayor had the police shoot down the poor in the town square, and gave the rich 24 hours to get out of town. Using terror, political assassination, and well-conceived monopolies, Montiel became the richest man in town. His career is a case history of the period known as *la violencia*, paralleling the last years of the 1940s (Montiel died in 1951).[25] As was often the case with wealthy families, the Montiel children were sent to Europe during this time of chaos. From Paris the two daughters write, "It's impossible to live in a country so savage that people are killed for political reasons" (*CS*, 153). The son who commissioned Balthazar to make him a bird cage (in the earlier story) writes from his consular post in Germany that he does not dare return for fear he will be shot in reprisal for his father's actions.

The havoc brought about by Montiel's outrageous conduct is symptomatic of the national malaise during this difficult period in Colombian history.

Melvin S. Arrington, Jr., views Montiel's widow as a metaphor of the society she represents.[26] She is dominated by superstition (Carmichael, a family friend, always enters the house with his umbrella open) and nearly loses her mind as she stares out at the interminable rains of October. Amid the ruins around her, Montiel's widow has a vision of the legendary Big Mama that foretells her death. This detail is important, for Big Mama is the central figure in the title story of the collection and the grand matriarch of Macondo and the entire ecclesiastical world. Here she is described as an apparition, wearing a white sheet, with a comb in her lap, and squashing lice with her thumbs. "When am I going to die?" the widow asks Big Mama. "When the tiredness begins in your arm," she replies (*CS*, 153). Linker believes this statement is the prediction of the widow's death, as well as the death of her social class, signaled when the will to rule—the strength in her arm—has been exhausted (Linker, 90). The decline and collapse of Montiel's materialistic world are envisioned here by García Márquez as an augury of a future world governed by socialism.

"One Day after Saturday"

One of the longer and more enigmatic stories in this volume is "Un día después del sábado" ("One Day after Saturday"). It won a prize in 1955 from the Association of Colombian Artists and Writers, a fact that indicates the approximate date it was written. It is set in Macondo at a time when the period of decadence had already begun, and its principal characters are Rebecca and Father Antonio Isabel Santísimo Sacramento del Altar Castañeda y Montero, both of whom appear later in *One Hundred Years of Solitude*. Rebecca was first seen briefly in *Leaf Storm* and later in "Tuesday Siesta." Father Anthony Isabel was an important figure in *In Evil Hour* and later in "Big Mama's Funeral."

As is frequently the case in García Márquez's fiction, this short story is built around the premise of the sudden appearance of an unusual phenomenon that breaks down the sense of order in society. Here it is a veritable plague of dead birds that throws life in Macondo into turmoil. First Rebecca's house is invaded by the birds. When she reports the incident to the mayor, she finds his desk piled high with his own dead birds. Father Anthony Isabel, now 94 and reputedly senile, pays little attention to the phenomenon at first, and only becomes interested when a bird falls at his feet as he passes Rebecca's house. Their attempt to revive it fails, but this incident causes the priest to consider the episode more seriously. By means of free association he at first considers the event to be a work of Satan and therefore a prelude to the Apocalypse. Then he jumps to the conclusion that the occurrence is somehow related to the biblical story of the Wandering Jew who brought devastation wherever he went and was condemned to roam until Christ's Second Coming.

All of this occurs in the priest's mind as he makes his way to the railroad station to meet the afternoon train. On this day the train has only 4 cars, but he can remember when it once had 140, all loaded with bananas, and took the entire afternoon to pass through Macondo. He continues to come to the station every afternoon, "even after they shot the workers to death and the banana plantations were finished . . . and there was left only that yellow, dusty train which neither brought anyone nor took anyone away" (*CS*, 165). The last sentence is an obvious reference to one of the major incidents in *One Hundred Years of Solitude* and demonstrates that as early as 1955 García Márquez had a skeletal outline in mind for the masterpiece published 12 years later. While some of the dates in Macondo's fictitious history as presented here do not coincide with those given earlier in *Leaf Storm*, what is important is that by 1955 the general form Macondo was to take was already in existence.

Father Anthony Isabel's Wandering Jew theory takes on a life of its own when a young boy gets off the train for a quick lunch but misses the train's early departure. The boy is from the provincial town of Manaure, and sees electricity for the first time in Macondo. After a fitful sleep in Macondo's only hotel, he decides, since it is Sunday, to attend mass. The priest notices him in the small congregation, notes that he is wearing a hat, and draws an ambiguous relationship between the boy and the Wandering Jew. The puzzled congregation thinks Father Anthony Isabel has gone crazy, especially when he asks the acolyte to take up an offering and give it to the boy so that he can buy a new hat. This enigmatic conclusion to the story fails to clarify the exact meaning of the disparate events in it. Whether the Wandering Jew is a vision, a dream, or an invention by the priest is never clarified. The focus of the story is on religion and the ineffectiveness of Father Anthony Isabel and the church in the daily life of Macondo. At the end of the story nothing has happened to explain the phenomenon of the dead birds or the reasons the priest had to relate the story of the Wandering Jew to the young boy who missed his train.

"Artificial Roses"

In this short story ("Rosas artificiales") three of the major characters from *In Evil Hour* reappear, as does the motif of dead mice in the church. Father Angel, who will not let women with bare-shouldered dresses take Communion, is mentioned. While his dress code shapes the course of the narrative, he has no active role in the story. Attention focuses on Mina, a young girl caught between the miasma of small-town life and the intrusive meddling of her blind grandmother. As she prepares for Friday mass, she discovers that her grandmother washed the detachable sleeves of the dress she planned to wear. Fully aware of Father Angel's inflexible attitude and wearing her sleeveless dress, she leaves for mass in a huff, only to return a quarter-hour later.

Although blind, the grandmother is able to "see" a great deal: she realizes that Mina never intended to attend mass with the sleeveless dress and that she made an unusual second visit to the bathroom upon her return. (The reader knows that the second visit was to dispose of a packet of letters written on colored paper.) At this point Mina's friend, Trinidad, arrives to help her make 1,800 artificial roses for Easter. She brings with her a shoe box filled with the dead mice caught in the church traps the night before. When the grandmother overhears Mina whisper to Trinidad, "He went away," she understands Mina's unusual behavior as the result of a broken love affair and not anger over the damp sleeves that prevented her from taking Communion. As the story ends, Mina screams an obscenity at her grandmother for her meddling, and the old lady replies, "I'm crazy . . . [b]ut apparently you haven't thought of sending me to the madhouse so long as I don't start throwing stones" (*CS*, 183).

Implicit in this story is the conflict between exterior appearance and the interior self, especially in religious matters. Mina's detachable sleeves give the appearance of piety during Communion, but they can quickly be removed once she is outside the church. Her trade in artificial roses is another clue to her emphasis on exterior appearance. Her attempt to camouflage a broken love affair is thwarted by the perceptive grandmother, who believes it is a sacrilege to take Communion when one is angry. The grandmother is forced by her blindness to live in an inner world where appearance does not count. While Mina dedicates herself to the interminable task of making artificial roses, the grandmother tends the natural roses growing in their patio.

Enrique Sacerio-Garí concludes that such a comparison between what is real and what is illusory in this story is inevitable.[27] Taking the analogy a step further, he believes the reader must carry the process to its logical end: the ultimate artifice is the printed page containing the story "Artificial Roses" that the reader holds in his hands. In an exercise worthy of Jorge Luis Borges, García Márquez takes the reader from the interior (real) world of the grandmother to Mina's artificial world of appearance (paper roses) to the ultimate artifice of all (the printed page containing the story).

The use of a rose as symbol is seen again in the final paragraphs of the story. Still angry and resentful, Mina is left with "a fistful of unfinished stems and roses" (*CS*, 182). Her mother, hearing the exchange of harsh words, comes along the corridor with "her arms full of bouquets of [real] thorned flowers" (*CS*, 183). The unpleasant thorns of inner reality, then, must be valued above the artificial, unfinished world of guise.

"Big Mama's Funeral"

If all of García Márquez's writings up to this point are considered a preamble to his more recent masterpieces, then "Los funerales de la Mamá Grande" ("Big Mama's Funeral") is the first opus of his mature canon. Many critics believe it is his most accomplished piece of short fiction, and it has been more widely examined than any of his other short stories. Placed at the end of the collection that carries its name as a general title, it is both a précis of the seven previous stories and a precursor of future masterpieces and stylistic innovations.

The short opening paragraph alerts the reader to the presence of hyperbolic humor that is to be a hallmark of some of his most successful fiction: "This is, for all the world's unbelievers, the true account of Big Mama, absolute sovereign of the Kingdom of Macondo, who lived for ninety-two years, and died in the odor of sanctity one Tuesday last September and whose funeral was attended by the Pope" (*CS*, 184). Within this single sentence the door is opened to a world of florid exaggeration and satiric comedy within the framework of the folktale, and the daring exaggeration of its rhetoric ultimately creates a myth of enormous proportions. García Márquez uses the tale to lambaste political, social, and religious institutions, as well as the Colombian semifeudal system of land tenure. At the same time the author takes giant steps forward in the conceptualization of the fictionalized reader, called the *narrataire* by David William Foster.[28] Big Mama is the prototype of the protagonist of *The Autumn of the Patriarch* and shares many of the Rabelaisian characteristics evident in *One Hundred Years of Solitude*.

Now that Macondo has returned to relative calm, the chronicler is eager to offer a detailed version of the commotion "before the historians have a chance to get at it" (*CS*, 185). After the bombastic opening paragraph, the story can be divided into two segments. In the first the narrator relates the events regarding the final illness of Big Mama and paints a picture of the semifeudal political and social conditions in Macondo. Fourteen weeks before her demise she orders her attendants to seat her in her rattan rocker so that she can put the affairs of her soul in order with the help of Father Anthony Isabel (seen earlier in "One Day after Saturday"), then dictates her last testament. Her domain is worthy of a feudal lord: five townships where 352 families live as tenant farmers, annually paying her rent, tribute, and tithes. Her empire is a modern-day latifundium typically found in many parts of Spanish America as the result of the colonial *encomienda* system.[29]

Big Mama requires three hours to enumerate her earthly possessions, after which she begins to detail her immaterial effects: "[t]he wealth of the subsoil, the territorial waters, the colors of the flag, national sovereignty, the traditional parties, the rights of man, civil rights, . . . free elections, beauty queens, transcendental speeches, . . . the Supreme Court, goods whose importation was forbidden, liberal ladies . . . the free but responsible press, the Athens of South America [a name given Bogotá], public opinion, the lessons of democracy, Christian morality, . . . the Communist menace, the ship of state" (*CS*, 192). But before she can finish, she emits a loud belch and expires. The list is a tongue-in-cheek registry of platitudes and makes fun of lofty legalistic language and journalistic clichés.

Her expiration marks the midpoint of the chronicle. The second half describes the consternation her death causes in the entire nation, as well as in the ecclesiastical world. The news even reaches the Vatican, and the pope makes plans to visit Macondo to attend her last rites. The president of the republic, where beggars wrapped in newspapers sleep in the shelter of the capitol, faces the "historic blahblahblah" of a congress debating whether he can visit Macondo for the funeral. The pope makes his way to the tropical fiefdom in a canoe filled with yucca, green bananas, and crates of chickens, but his first glimpse of a land filled with balsam apples and iguanas erases the suffering of his trip and compensates him for his sacrifice. The president's dilemma is resolved with the promulgation of the official decision that "Public Order was disturbed, ratatatat, and that the President of the Republic, ratatatat, had in his power the extraordinary prerogatives, ratatatat, which permitted him to attend Big Mama's funeral, ratatatat, tatatat, tatat, tatat" (*CS*, 197). Again García Márquez takes aim at official language and journalese.

In the interim Big Mama's corpse has been baking in 104-degree heat in the shade. Finally the great day arrives. The funeral has a carnivalesque quality, as great multitudes fill the streets while Big Mama's relatives and employees sack the abandoned mansion. A bald, chubby, old, and ailing president; a delegation of archbishops; and a cluster of military officers represent the nation's power structure. And then there are the beauty queens and many "others who are omitted so as not to make this account interminable" (*CS*, 199). Here the narrator addresses the fictionalized reader, whose attention may be lagging. No one noticed the buzzards flying above the cortege or the pestilential garbage the hordes left behind in Macondo's streets. A thunderous sigh of relief marks the end of the funeral ceremony, and Big Mama's tomb is sealed with a lead plinth.

Now, the narrator concludes, the pope can ascend to heaven in body and soul, the president can sit and govern, and the beauty queens can marry and have many sons. The only thing left is for the storyteller to lean a stool against the doorway and to narrate this story so that no disbeliever will be left who does not know the tale of Big Mama. There is a certain urgency in his tone, "because tomorrow, Wednesday, the garbage men will come and will sweep away the garbage from her funeral, forever and ever" (*CS*, 200).

This story is dominated by obvious hyperbolic humor that reaches the level of satire. Roger M. Peel believes this sense of humor sets García Márquez apart from other contemporary Spanish American writers, and allows him to humanize a world in which corruption, poverty, violence, and suffering would otherwise produce only pessimistic despair.[30] The key to its humor is exaggeration, exaggeration of Big Mama's empire and of the disproportionate obsequies at her death. The result is the invention of a myth of gigantic proportions. Williams describes this invention as the product of García Márquez's characterization of Big Mama as a truly extraordinary type, a characterization that places her a legendary realm beyond everyday reality of cause-and-effect relationships (Williams, 45). Her realm is both mythical and magical and points the way to magical realism, a literary technique that is common in contemporary Spanish American fiction and that blends reality and fantasy in the creation of a new level of realism operating outside commonly accepted parameters. While this is not the first time magical realism has appeared in García Márquez's writings, it is the first instance in which it permeates the entire work.

The world created by the magical-realist framework of "Big Mama's Funeral" is one in which the reader must accept the improbability of a visit from the pope to the distant realm of Macondo. García Márquez claims that in Spanish America fantasy often anticipates reality, and some years after the publication of this tale Pope Paul VI did indeed visit Colombia. When García Márquez originally wrote the story, he consciously changed the appearance of the president of the republic to avoid any comparison with Colombia's president at the time. But when the papal visit did occur, the new president fit the description in the short story almost perfectly (Peel, 165–66).

Judith Goetzinger affirms that the single theme underlying and co-ordinating the diverse elements in this narrative is that of decay, a social and moral disintegration in the first half of the story, and actual decomposition in the second half.[31] The decadence of Big Mama's domain is embodied by the doddering old priest, Father Anthony Isabel, as well as by the incestuous relationships within Big Mama's family clan. Closely related to the idea of decay is the myth of power that has grown about her. But the myth of her power is eventually divested of its might, a victim of her own exaggerations and excesses.

A major contribution of this story is its fictionalization of the reader. Here Foster posits not one but two readers or *narrataires* (Foster, 104). The first reader is concerned with the many forms of official language the text includes and may be considered the traditional, uncritical reader. The second reader is one who is "able to gauge the distance between official history, folk legend, and demythifying literature. In short, the reader who is able implicitly to discover the ways in which the purported raconteur's tale is not the exegesis of legend . . . but the demythification of both legend and official history" (Foster, 104). Williams points out that this story is successful because it fictionalizes a reader whose role many readers find appealing to assume (Williams, 46).

A secondary motif present in this story is García Márquez's interest in Tuesday, the day of the week around which the tale revolves. Earlier, the superstitious belief that Tuesday is an unpropitious day to marry, to take a trip, or to leave one's family appeared in "Tuesday Siesta." Here Big Mama's death happens "one Tuesday last September" (*CS*, 184). The *narrataire* tells his tale of a Tuesday because "tomorrow, Wednesday, the garbage men will come" to sweep up the wastes forever (*CS*, 200). Big Mama's death and subsequently her funeral both occur on the same inauspicious day of the week, thereby substantiating the proverbial injunction.

"Big Mama's Funeral" anticipates *One Hundred Years of Solitude* in its creation of myth, its use of hyperbolic humor, and its emphasis on the role of the storyteller. In the opinion of Robert Sims, this story "represents freedom and discovery: freedom to create the myth of Macondo and discovery of the techniques to achieve it.[32] Big Mama in her role as protagonist likewise anticipates the despot of *The Autumn of the Patriarch*, whose gross exaggerations nearly destroy his unnamed Caribbean nation. Both novels offer a meditation on the solitude of absolute power, an idea suggested by Big Mama herself. Magical realism, so prominently seen in this short story, informs both of the novels that follow it.

Big Mama's Funeral contains eight examples of García Márquez's short fiction. Each story focuses on an individual in a crumbling society where it is impossible to establish solidarity with other human beings, and the future offers no hope (Goetzinger, 244–45). Only in the last story, which gives the collection its title, is there a marked departure in both language and style. These changes are important, for they represent the shape and form of the writer's future fiction and his ability to create the magical or mythical dimension (Goetzinger, 246). After finishing the incredible tale of Big Mama, the reader is forced back into the mundane world of social reality, for tomorrow, Wednesday, the street sweepers, and with them the historians, will take over Macondo.

Innocent Eréndira:
Humor and Entertainment

With the 1967 publication of *One Hundred Years of Solitude* and its unprecedented popularity in Spanish America, Europe, and the United States, García Márquez passed from the ranks of a secondary writer to the spotlight of critical attention and the furor of public interest. Following the initial success of this novel, critics began to evaluate his earlier short stories and novels in terms of this popular masterpiece. Various collections of his earlier short stories and newspaper articles began to appear, and in 1972 his most recent volume of short stories came out with the unusually long title *La increíble y triste historia de la cándida Eréndira y de su abuela desalmada (The Incredible and Sad Tale of Innocent Eréndira and Her Heartless Grandmother)*. It contains seven short stories that represent the work of a mature artist who seeks to entertain with well-written tales designed for readers of all ages.

The original dates of publication of these seven stories cover a time span from 1961 to 1972. As was the case with the collection *Big Mama's Funeral,* the title story contains many reappearing characters from earlier stories in the volume. Throughout the series magical realism, humor, and even certain elements of optimism are evident. This collection represents a transition from the fiction of Macondo (which ended with *One Hundred Years of Solitude*) to central themes later seen in his most recent fiction: exploitation on both a personal and a national scale, the extraordinary power of the human imagination, and the use of the sea as an enduring metaphor. But the emphasis in these short stories is to entertain, and the raucous humor first seen in the tale "Big Mama's Funeral" reaches a high level of development in this volume.

As Regina Janes has indicated, the texts in this collection resist interpretation and are written "in a wholly symbolic mode . . . to repel the impertinence of any interpretations imposed upon them through the intransigence of the irreducible, impenetrable events or images at the center. While a great deal may be said about these stories, they have been designed to escape the critic's web of exegesis."[33] Another significant factor is that the stories are not arranged in exact chronological order, thereby suggesting that they were ordered in such a way as to elaborate thematic development. There is little dialogue in these stories, and all are related by an omniscient narrator to readers who must be willing to accept a universe in which everything is possible. That two of the tales first appeared with the subtitle "A Story for Children" makes the point that the reader must accept a world of the marvelous, not unlike the world of Macondo with its remarkable magical qualities.

In an insightful essay Mark Millington suggests a frame of reference within which all of the stories in the collection take place:

> Each story in [this collection] begins with an arrival—a space of a consciousness is invaded by an unknown presence. But the nature of the invading presence differs. . . . [I]n four of the stories the source of the invading presence is the same: in one way or another, the sea is associated with the arrival . . . [a]nd in all of the stories the arrival has the same extraordinary effect. . . . [It] represents the inception of a series of events that will occupy the remainder of the story. The effect of the arrival is to disrupt. . . . The interest stimulated by the new arrival centres on a common reaction in several stories: the need to discover the meaning of the disruption. But the invading presence also seems to produce a release of energy in the characters and to create a new pattern of life.[34]

Millington determines that in most of these stories a kind of carnivalization takes place; such a process serves to amplify the effect of the new arrivals (Millington, 119–21). The amorphous structure of these tales does not sustain forward plot movement to a culminating conclusion. Most of these short stories end with the departure of the invading presence, after which life may either continue as it was before the arrival or be indelibly altered as a result of the event. In any case, the carnival is over, but the potential for change that it offered is a welcome hiatus in everyday life, even if the change lasts only for the duration of the festivity.

"A Very Old Man with Enormous Wings"

This 1968 "tale for children" ("Un señor muy veijo con unas alas enormes") fits Millington's formula for this collection almost perfectly.

Its thesis is the arrival, in a poor coastal town, of an old man with wings. Thought to be an angel by some, he is considered a circus freak by his hosts, Pelayo and Elisenda, and by most of the villagers. Since he speaks an unknown tongue, the theories concerning his origin abound. A large crowd gathers around the chicken coop where his hosts have placed him, and the entire episode becomes a carnival when they decide to charge admission to view him.

The local priest, Father Gonzaga, alarmed at the news, arrives early the next day to attempt a solution to the problem. Since the old man does not respond to Latin, the priest judges him an impostor. But the curious come from afar to see the phenomenon, and a carnival arrives to take advantage of the large crowds. Father Gonzaga, in the meantime, sends a letter to the pope for clarification of the event. The Vatican wants to know whether the old man knows Aramaic, whether he could fit on the head of a pin, and whether he has a navel. Although he seems able to perform miracles, they are not the miracles desired. A blind man, for example, grows three new teeth.

The crowds begin to diminish when the carnival displays a woman who had been changed into an enormous spider for having attended a dance without parental permission. The incident of the spider woman frequently appears in other García Márquez writings, often serving as a symbol of exploitation. Nevertheless, Pelayo and Elisenda have profited greatly from their enterprise. They now have an elaborate new home, and Elisenda has been able to purchase satin shoes and silk dresses. The angel, however, has taken over their life and home: "it was awful living in that hell full of angels" (*CS*, 209). Yet one morning, as Elisenda was cutting onions for lunch, she saw the angel attempting to fly. Slowly he began to gain altitude; she let out a sigh of relief as he ceased to be "an arrogance in her life but an imaginary dot on the horizon of the sea" (*CS*, 210).

The arrival-carnivalization-departure formula is readily apparent in this story. It also offers a series of possible interpretations, none of which is ever confirmed; the story successfully resists exegesis but at the same time centers the reader's attention on the power of human imagination. In the end the old man is but "an imaginary dot on the horizon," a dot whose very existence defies the human rational world.

The first lines of the tale set a biblical tone: "[o]n the third day of rain they had killed so many crabs inside the house that Pelayo had to cross his drenched courtyard and throw them into the sea" (*CS*, 203).

It is not, however, until the reader reaches the last word of the last sentence in the opening paragraph that the narrator reveals the magical realism of the situation: "it was an old man, a very old man, lying face down in the mud, who, in spite of his tremendous efforts, couldn't get up, impeded by his enormous wings" (*CS*, 203). The idea of wings, expressed in the last word of the paragraph, suddenly opens the narrative to myriad possibilities. There is no moment of closure that identifies the writer's intentions. While it has been suggested that the angel's departure is the result of his disillusion with the promotional exploitation surrounding his visit, García Márquez at no time suggests this intent.[35] Rather, he clearly states that what he seeks to explore in this so-called children's story is the free reign of the imagination (Mendoza, 31). Coming as it does at the beginning of the collection, it sets the stage for subsequent stories that range from the magical to the imaginary. For this reason "A Very Old Man with Enormous Wings" is a fitting first story in the *Innocent Eréndira* collection.

"The Sea of Lost Time"

The date of this story ("El mar del tiempo perdido," 1961) sets it apart from the rest of the collection; in fact, it appeared after García Márquez had published his first two novels, and precedes *One Hundred Years of Solitude* by six years. It is interesting as a landmark in the development of the author's method and style, and it is one of the first examples of his using the liberating power of the human imagination in the creation of fiction. Set in an arid coastal town similar to many on the Guajira Peninsula, the tale opens with the invasion of an enigmatic fragrance of roses, something practically unknown in the region. Tobías is the first person in the village to notice the smell, and he discusses it with Clotilde, his skeptical wife. Petra, an older neighbor, believes it presages her death and asks her husband, Jacob, to bury her alive on land to assure her that she will not be thrown into the sea. Shortly thereafter she does die, and the customary sea burial occurs despite her wishes.

With the spread of the news of the fragrance of roses, large crowds come and turn village life into a carnival. In the crowd is Mr. Herbert, reputedly the richest man in the world, who dispenses largesse at a price to the poor inhabitants. Life becomes a fiesta. A poor boy who needs 48 pesos must imitate 48 birdcalls, and a girl who needs 500 pesos must make love to 100 men at 5 pesos each. Mr. Herbert dazzles the inhabitants with the exciting possibility of turning the town into a city with tall glass buildings. In the meantime, he wins Jacob's house in a game of checkers and then falls asleep for days.

Mr. Herbert is the same person who totally changed the face of Macondo in *One Hundred Years of Solitude* when he initiated the invasion of the banana company. He is the symbol of North American exploitation, and, as Williams observes, "[h]is token gifts, false goodwill, promises of a splendid future, and acquisition of the town's property are all characteristics of the manipulations of foreign capitalists in the early fiction" (Williams, 100). But it is the story's ending that is stylistically important. As Mr. Herbert sleeps and the fragrance of roses disappears, the crowds begin to leave, and the town is again the same as it was before. When Mr. Herbert wakes up, "[t]he rain had fermented the garbage the crowds had left in the streets and the soil was arid and hard as a brick once more" (*CS*, 226). At this point he invites Tobías, the first one in the village to smell the roses, to accompany him to the depths of the sea. There they swim by a submerged village with brightly colored flowers and enter the sea of the dead, where they see Petra, now 50 years younger. Mr. Herbert cautions Tobías not to mention this experience to anyone; "[j]ust imagine the disorder there'd be in the world if people found out about these things" (*CS*, 228). After his return to the village Tobías does attempt to share some of these experiences with Clotilde, but she dismisses him with the words, "for the love of God, don't start up with those things again" (*CS*, 229).

Tobías's vision of a world of fantasy and imagination, seen here for the first time in García Márquez's fiction, will later be the hallmark of the Macondo fiction and subsequent writings. The tone of the narrative, described as "humorous, mock-omniscient, warm, exuberant, witty, very winsom," points the way to the dominant purpose of the story: to achieve a high mark in the art of storytelling.[36]

"The Handsomest Drowned Man in the World"

This short story ("El ahogado más hermoso del mundo," 1968), allegedly written for children, uses the formula already seen in "A Very Old Man with Enormous Wings." Set in a barren coastal village, the tale recounts the sudden appearance of the body of an enormous drowned man on the nearby shore, and its impact on men, women, and children. As the story moves ahead, both the nature of the village and that of the drowned man are gradually revealed.[37] The children first discover the body, and play with it all afternoon. The adults, alarmed by the inexplicable anomaly, carry the body to the nearest house. At this point the respective roles of the men and women diverge. While the men visit neighboring villages to find out whether anyone is missing, the women clean the body and are amazed at the visitor's size, appearance, and virility. They fantasize about his past life and secretly compare him with their own men. Finally, they realize he is so exceptional that "there was no room for him in their imagination" (*CS*, 231). They agree that his name must be Esteban (Stephen).

When the men return with the news that he is not from a neighboring village, the women jubilantly proclaim him theirs. Some natural jealousy develops between the men and women, but all join together in the task of clothing him and preparing a magnificent funeral, resplendent with flowers and honorary family members chosen from the ranks of the villagers. After the burial in the sea, Esteban's memory causes the inhabitants to rebuild houses, plant flowers on the cliffs, and paint their village with bright colors, for now they realize they are incomplete without Esteban. He stimulated their imaginations to look beyond the emptiness of their lives and to envision a new life for their village. They will plant flowers on the rocky cliffs, and travelers on cruise ships will awaken to "the smell of gardens on the high seas;" ship captains will say in 14 languages, "[O]ver there, where the sun's so bright . . . yes, over there, that's Esteban's village" (*CS*, 236).

The carnivalization formula, used earlier with respect to the first story in this collection, serves to define this story as well. In both cases an enigmatic visitor changes the entire routine of village life; both visits cause a carnivalesque celebration—an elaborate funeral, in the case of the second story. Both visitors ultimately depart, but in the second story there is a feeling of optimism, and the idea that change is feasible is implicit in the tale's open-ended conclusion. Mary E. Davis concludes that "[t]he meaning of the story must be developed in the mind of the reader, for it is not readily apparent from the various elements of the plot" (Davis, 160). The idea of purification by baptism in the sea and the ultimate rebirth of the village after Esteban's departure are clearly present.

A Faulknerian technique used here with great success consists of shifting the narrative point of view and the speaker within a single sentence, as is the case of the imagined dialogue between a high-strung hostess and an uncomfortable Esteban eager to please:

They could see him in life, condemned to going through doors sideways, cracking his head on crossbeams, remaining on his feet during visits, not knowing what to do with his soft, pink, sea lion hands while the lady of the house looked for her most resistant chair and begged him, frightened to death, sit here, Esteban, please, and he, leaning against the wall, smiling, don't bother, ma'am, I'm fine where I am, his heels raw and his back roasted from having done the same thing so many times whenever he paid a visit, don't bother, ma'am, I'm fine where I am, just to avoid the embarrassment of breaking up the chair, and never knowing perhaps that the ones who said don't go, Esteban, at least wait till the coffee's ready, were the ones who later on would whisper the big boob finally left, how nice, the handsome fool has gone. (*CS*, 233)

Such shifting of narrative point of view in midsentence later becomes a common occurrence in *The Autumn of the Patriarch*, stylistically García Márquez's most Faulknerian novel. The novel's last chapter, some 50 pages long, consists of a single sentence with innumerable shifts of narrator and perspective.

The timing of the action in this short story is important for its thematic relationship to the idea of Esteban as a classical hero. The action begins inauspiciously on a Tuesday marked by rough seas, but after midnight "the sea fell into its Wednesday drowsiness" (*CS*, 233). Esteban's mysterious arrival, gargantuan size, and unusual beauty are all marks of heroic, superhuman stature. The name given him by the women suggests comparison with the martyr St. Stephen, "a man full of faith and of the Holy Spirit" (Acts 6:5). Esteban's dynamic presence is also his message, and his funeral rites are worthy of any hero. Davis relates the drowned man's name to James Joyce's creations, Stephen Hero and Stephen Dedalus, and draws a parallel between Joyce's use of art to create other realities and to critique reality and García Márquez's use of art to show the psychic possibilities of human imagination (Davis, 166–67). St. Stephen's martyrdom stimulated the growth of a new Christian era just as Esteban's visit allows the villagers to open their imagination to the creation of new ideas to replenish their solitary town.

"Death Constant beyond Love"

The title of this story ("Muerte constante más allá del amor," 1970) is the reversal of the title of a sonnet by the seventeenth-century Spanish poet and satirist Francisco de Quevedo. Quevedo's title, "Amor constante más allá de la muerte" (Love constant beyond death), focuses on the eternal quality of love, but García Márquez places emphasis on the incessant ability of death to negate love.[38] The story's outline relates the visit of Senator Onésimo Sánchez to the desert village Rosal del Virrey (Rosebush of the Viceroy), known primarily as a haven for smugglers' ships. Sánchez is in the midst of a reelection campaign, but secretly his doctors have told him he will be dead by Christmas. The senator observes the masses of Indians and townspeople assembled to hear his memorized speech. As he talks, his assistants erect cardboard buildings to depict what Rosal del Virrey will become if he is reelected. Even a cardboard ocean liner is made to pass in front of the red brick facades of the make-believe houses.

Absent from the political event is an old acquaintance, Nelson Farina, an escapee from the Devil's Island prison. Farina is the father of a beautiful daughter, Laura, but he desperately needs a fake identity card, something the senator has previously refused to obtain. This time, however, Farina sends Laura as a token payment for this favor. She is dressed in her best clothes, but the politician discovers she is wearing a chastity belt under her dress, and her father has the key. Laura offers to retrieve it, but Sánchez tells her to stay "and sleep awhile. . . . It's good to be with someone when you're so alone" (*CS*, 245). Six months and 11 days later he in fact does die in the arms of Laura Farina. He has been repudiated because of the public scandal his affair has caused, and he dies in a rage because death is a constant, inescapable factor beyond the passionate love he has for Laura.

Within the story the idea of death and solitude is ever present. When Sánchez discovers that he and Laura are both Aries, he announces, "It's the sign of solitude" (*CS*, 244). Aries is, in fact, not the sign of solitude but rather a symbol of the creative impulse and of the spirit at the moment of its inception. Sánchez conveniently changes its meaning to coincide with his present situation. His solitude is the solitude of power, an idea central to the novel *The Autumn of the Patriarch*. Rei Berroa suggests the senator's age of 42 coincides with the age of García Márquez when the story first appeared in 1970.[39] (Since the correct year of García Márquez's birth is in fact 1927, he would have been 43.) The solitude of the senator may be a reflection of the solitude of García Márquez, who was forced to separate himself from an adulatory public after the 1967 publication of *One Hundred Years of Solitude*. Sánchez is faced with the difficult choice between his future political career and his infatuation with Laura Farina. Certain death eventually will end both options; he chooses Laura.

Exploitation is another central idea in "Death Constant beyond Love." There is a dual exploitation: Nelson Farina is willing to sacrifice his daughter for the favor of false identification papers, and Senator Onésimo Sánchez willingly uses cardboard houses as a ploy to deceive a gullible public. Sánchez's circus equals the exploitative gestures of Mr. Herbert in "The Sea of Lost Time" and mirrors the subterfuge of the charlatan Blacamán, the protagonist of another short story, published in 1968. At one point Nelson Farina says in French, "C'est le Blacamán de la politique" ("He's the Blacamán of politics") (*CS*, 241). Farina's pejorative description of the senator reflects the low level Sánchez's campaign has reached.

An important motif in this story is the rose Senator Sánchez wears throughout his visit. Despite its name, the dusty village of Rosal del Virrey can grow practically nothing in its hot, saltpeter soil. Laura confesses that she once saw a rose, but in Riohacha, the departmental capital. Rosal del Virrey's only "rose" is Laura Farina, and her father readily allows the senator to pick it. Laura is the rose that will illumine the senator's solitude for the next six months. But Laura is doomed to solitude as well; the senator will most certainly die, and his radiant German wife and five children will inherit his estate.

"Last Voyage of the Ghost Ship"

"El último viaje del buque fantasma" (1968; "Last Voyage of the Ghost Ship") is an anomaly in this collection; it consists of a single sentence in a single paragraph, extending to some six pages. It is a tour de force that presages the style and method of *The Autumn of the Patriarch* and is a veritable paean to the power of the human imagination. The story is told by an omniscient narrator, but shifts to other speakers occur frequently. This one-sentence narrative relates the recurring vision of a boy who has seen a transatlantic cruise ship pass by his coastal village, disappearing when the light of the nearby beacon strikes its side, then reappearing shortly before it runs into the shoals and silently sinks. The colonial city on the other side of the bay where the action takes place is Cartagena de Indias, the historic seaport on Colombia's northern coast celebrated in the novel *Love in the Time of Cholera*.

When the vision recurs a year later, the boy shares the experience with his mother, who believes he has gone mad. The following year he takes her to the bay to see the sight for herself, but she dies during the event. Forced to depend on public charity and theft to survive, the boy, now a young man, waits another year; when the ghost ship approaches again, he runs into the streets to alert the town's inhabitants. No one sees the ship, and the villagers "covered him with blows and left him so twisted that it was then he said to himself . . . now they're going to see who I am" (*CS*, 249). His determination pays off a year later; when the enormous ship appears, he guides it by means of a red lantern in a small boat. It is "bigger than any other big thing in the world and darker than any other dark thing on land or sea" (*CS*, 249). He guides it to the shoreline, where it crashes before the very eyes of the town's disbelievers. This happens on a Tuesday night and is followed by a radiant Wednesday morning during which the stunned villagers contemplate the wrecked ocean liner aground in front of the church. Remarkably, the vessel is 20 times taller than the church steeple and 97 times longer than the village itself. Engraved on the bow in iron letters is the ship's name, *Halálcsillag* (*Death Star*, in Hungarian), an ominous yet ironic name in view of the fact that Hungary has no fleet of ocean liners. This name may well be a carefully designed ploy on the part of García Márquez, who frequently objects to the critics' propensity to overinterpret.

Hyperbolic descriptions of the event and of the cruise ship itself dominate the concluding lines of this tale. Like others in the collection, the story contains the idea of the invasion of the village by a gigantic presence, in this case a phantasmagoric ship. Its arrival totally disrupts village life, with extraordinary consequences. The anomaly, however, is that the shipwreck is a product of the young man's will and imagination, employed here in an effort to affirm his worth in the eyes of the community.

The story's structure includes the idea of an arrival and of a carnivalization in reverse (the shipwreck), but its climactic ending fails to include a departure motif (Millington, 123). The use of a single sentence suggests the idea of the boy's obsession (Janes, 81). His ability to will the existence of the cruise ship stands as a cenotaph to the human imagination. Finally, García Márquez again uses Tuesday as the unpropitious day of the week for the culmination of the action. Although the story's coda, set on a radiant Wednesday morning, stands apart as the narrator contemplates his final victory over the disbelievers, perhaps the author's greatest achievement in "Last Voyage of the Ghost Ship" is his creation of a short story that resists definitive interpretation and exegesis.

"Blacamán the Good, Vendor of Miracles"

Reference to the title character, Blacamán, has already been noted in "Death Constant beyond Love," in which Senator Onésimo Sánchez is called "le Blacamán de la politique" (*CS*, 241). Blacamán will appear again in the 1972 title story of this collection, this time as a charlatan plying his trade on a gullible public. The name is a phonetic rendering in Spanish of the English words *black* and *man* as pronounced in so-called banana English, commonly heard in the Caribbean. "Blacamán el bueno vendedor de milagros" (1968) is narrated by Blacamán the Good, who tells the story of his original master, Blacamán the Bad, an unscrupulous confidence man in the imaginary port town of Santa María del Darién.

The tale begins on a Palm Sunday, when the narrator first meets the immortal huckster "with his white suspenders that were back stitched with gold thread, his rings with colored stones on every finger, and his braids of jingle bells" (*CS*, 252). Blacamán the Bad is demonstrating an antidote for bites of snakes, tarantulas, and centipedes. He successfully fakes a bite by a deadly bushmaster, rolls in agony, and miraculously recovers. The ploy is so successful that the antidote is quickly sold out, while marines from a cruiser from the North take color pictures of the event with telephoto lenses. This reference to the U.S. Marines introduces them in pejorative terms; they have been docked in Santa María for 20 years on a goodwill mission. The commander of the cruiser even buys the antidote; later when he tries to repeat the experiment in Philadelphia, he is changed into a glob of jelly in front of his staff. In an act of vengeance the marines invade the country under the pretext of exterminating yellow fever and end up killing "the natives, out of precaution, [and] also the Chinese, for distraction, the Negroes, from habit, and the Hindus, because they were snake charmers" (*CS*, 256).

Both Blacamáns are forced to flee into the desert of the Guajira, where they hide in a colonial mission. Blacamán the Bad, in a fit of pique, tortures his young protégé by hanging him by his ankles in the glaring sun and pulling out his fingernails. The young man reacts and grabs a rabbit carcass, throwing it against the wall. The carcass is revived, and the young Blacamán the Good acquires miraculous powers and becomes a healer himself. He journeys up and down the littoral, eventually acquiring an automobile, a Trinidadian chauffeur, and a chain of businesses that sell medals of his profile to tourists. When he later encounters his former master, he allows him to die in public, only to resuscitate him in a grandiose mausoleum, where, as punishment, he will live as long as Blacamán the Good, which, in the narrator's mind, is forever.

"Blacamán the Good, Vendor of Miracles" deals with exploitation, credulity, and the power of illusion in the towns along the Atlantic Coast and the dry, dusty reaches of the Guajira Peninsula (Janes, 72). It uses the technique suggested by Millington: arrival of the huckster/ carnival atmosphere of his activities/ultimate departure only to return. Abundant humor is interlaced with the phenomena of magical realism. The master-protégé paradigm recalls the classic picaresque tradition so common in sixteenth- and seventeenth-century Spanish literature. Unfavorable references to North American exploitation occur throughout the story. One perplexing problem is the question of historical time. McMurray calls this caprice "temporal contradictions and distortions" (McMurray, 123). Santa María del Darién, where the story begins, was a coastal town that did not survive the colonial era, yet the visit of the marines with cameras and telephoto lenses, and the presence of automobiles, makes the action twentieth century. Many of the coins mentioned in the narrative were used only in colonial times, and the first encounter of the two Blacamáns is dated "more than a century ago" (*CS*, 254).[40] Within the premises of magical realism such inconsistencies must be accepted so that the reader can focus on the events themselves.

The story is divided into seven long paragraphs, and a third of its sentences are more than 10 lines of text. Such sentences recall "Last Voyage of the Ghost Ship" (a single sentence) and the long paragraphs typical of *One Hundred Years of Solitude*. This technique will be characteristic of *The Autumn of the Patriarch*, published seven years after this short story. The narration often shifts from third to first person within the same sentence:

[W]ho dares say that I'm not a philanthropist, ladies and gentlemen, and now, yes, sir, commandant of the twentieth fleet, order your

47

boys to take down the barricades and let suffering humanity pass, lepers to the left, epileptics to the right, cripples where they won't get in the way, and there in the back the least urgent cases, only please don't crowd in on me because then I won't be responsible if the sicknesses get all mixed up and the people are cured of what they don't have, and keep the music playing until the brass boils, and rockets firing until the angels burn, and the liquor flowing until ideas are killed, and bring on the wenches and the acrobats . . . for here ends the evil fame of the Blacamáns and the universal tumult starts (*CS*, 259).

German D. Carrillo relates the theme of "Blacamán the Good, Vendor of Miracles" to events during and after Holy Week as recounted in the Bible (Carillo, 145–49). With the entry of Blacamán the Bad into Santa María, he fakes his death from snakebite, and women begin "laying blessed palms on top of him" (*CS*, 253). After the cruise commander's mishap with the antidote, both Blacamáns flee to the Guajira desert, reminiscent of Christ's time in the desert to escape persecution. With a change of roles, Blacamán the Good suffers a form of crucifixion when his mentor rolls him up in barbed wire, rubs salt into his wounds, and soaks him in brine. The miracle of the revived rabbit puts Blacamán the Good on the road to a career selling wondrous cures and potions. While the symbolism of Christ does inform the story, the final verdict must pronounce it a mock passion play in which two picaros deceive a credulous public.

"The Incredible and Sad Tale of Innocent Eréndira and Her Heartless Grandmother"

The incredible length of the mock-epic title of this 1972 novella ("La increíble y triste historia de la cándida Eréndira y de su abuela desalmada") recalls the cry of a huckster at a rural fair.[41] When one reads the novella as the last story in the collection, it is possible to see references to characters and situations in the first six. Divided into seven sections, the tale is told by an omniscient narrator up to the sixth section. At that point the narrative shifts to the first person; it is directed to a fictionalized reader and contains references to the Colombian musician Rafael Escalona and to García Márquez's close personal friend Alvaro Cepeda Samudio. Its central theme is the exploitation of Eréndira by her heartless grandmother, but there are suggestions of similar exploitation by the church, by foreign powers (most notably Spain and the United States), and by the military establishment.

In the opening section García Márquez paints a picture of malevolence on the part of the grandmother, who keeps Eréndira as a virtual slave in her enormous desert mansion. Fatigued from her endless chores, Eréndira forgets one night to extinguish the candelabra, and the "wind of her misfortune" makes it fall, causing a fire that destroys the house and her grandmother's belongings. Fourteen-year-old Eréndira is obliged to repay the entire debt by working as a prostitute. Clients, most of them military men, form long lines for her services. She and her grandmother move about from one town to another with a retinue of Indians, musicians, and a photographer, all of whom make up a veritable traveling circus.

When Eréndira meets Ulises, the handsome son of a Dutch farmer and an Indian woman, her life begins to change. They fall in love, and Eréndira for the first time is able to perceive life without brutal exploitation. Another change in her life occurs when she is kidnapped by nuns and placed in their convent to whitewash the stair steps. There she finally is happy; however, her grandmother pays an Indian boy to marry Eréndira during a mass convent wedding, and after taking the vows, she is free to leave and rejoin her grandmother.

Ulises and Eréndira attempt an abortive escape in his father's truck, but the grandmother shows the military authorities a letter of recommendation from Senator Onésimo Sánchez, and they catch the pair. Eréndira is forced once again into prostitution, but her grandmother makes the fatal error of telling her how she could someday be a person of power and influence. This sows the seeds of rebellion in her heart, and when Ulises appears again, she urges him to kill the grandmother. The grandmother survives first a poisoned birthday cake and then an explosion of dynamite in her piano. Finally, Ulises must stab her many times. She dies in a pool of green blood, but Eréndira "kept on running . . . beyond the arid winds and the never-ending sunsets and she was never heard of again nor was the slightest trace of her misfortune ever found" (*CS*, 311).

The relationship between the grandmother and Eréndira is the story's most obvious example of exploitation. Arnold M. Penuel suggests that in many ways the grandmother evokes Spain holding sway over its colonies.[42] The grandmother's husband, as well as her son

(Eréndira's father), is named Amadís, the same as the hero celebrated in the chivalric novel *Amadís de Gaula* (*Amadis of Gaule*). Penuel further states that the labors of Eréndira produce gold that the grandmother keeps in a vest worn under her blouse—a clear reference to the wealth of the New World that in colonial times went to Spain (Penuel, 71).

The paradigm of colonialism and exploitation produces a myth with both classical Greek prototypes and modern archetypes. Eréndira in the text of the story is called at one point Arídnere, the private name Ulises invented "when he wanted to think about her" (*CS*, 291). Arídnere is a variation of the Greek Ariadne, celebrated in the myth of the Minotaur as the damsel who fell in love with Theseus, the slayer of the monster (Penuel, 78). If Ulises is identified with Theseus, then the monster he slays represents the heartless grandmother. McMurray offers a modern reading of Eréndira as a form of the Spanish verb *rendir* ("to conquer" *or* "to surrender") plus an initial *e* (McMurray, 113). Both meanings of the verb relate to Eréndira's role in the story. Ulises is closely related in name and physical characteristics to the Homeric epic, but he never reaches the heroic stature of his namesake or that of Theseus. While he finally rescues Eréndira (Ariadne) by killing the grandmother (the Minotaur), it is he who is abandoned in the end when Eréndira keeps on running into the sunset. At one point Ulises refers to the grandmother as a white whale, perhaps a symbol of evil reminiscent of Melville's Moby-Dick (McMurray, 111). Finally, the frequent references to Ulises as *cara de ángel* (angel face) recall the character Miguel Cara de Angel in the classic *El señor presidente* (*Mr. President*), by the Guatemalan writer Miguel Angel Asturias (Janes, 86–87).

There is also a relationship between "Innocent Eréndira" and *Grimm's Fairy-Tales*, a correlation studied by Joel Hancock.[43] This relationship is replete with similar development of character, similar roles for cruelty and bloodshed, and a mixing of reality and fantasy.

This story is likewise related to other writings by García Márquez. Eréndira appears as a nameless victim in "The Sea of Lost Time," and the outline of the story's action is recounted as a short episode in *One Hundred Years of Solitude*. Previous stories in this collection are recalled by the references to Senator Onésimo Sánchez ("Death Constant beyond Love"), to Blacamán the Good, and to the spider woman ("A Very Old Man with Enormous Wings"). Williams believes that these cross-references provide a sense of wholeness for the fictionalized reader and allow that reader to reach a level of superiority over the characters depicted (Williams, 105).

Three motifs are present throughout the action: the wind, the desert, and the sea. From the very beginning it is Eréndira's "wind of misfortune" that causes the conflagration. During a fierce wind she is captured by the nuns and taken to the convent, and in the end she runs "beyond the arid winds" into the desert. The wind is thoroughly pervasive and serves as a symbol of her subjugation to nature and to fate (McNerney, 126). The sea and the desert are related motifs. Ulises tells Eréndira the sea is like the desert but with water, and his father once knew a man who could walk on water (*CS*, 278–79). Fernando Burgos believes both elements serve as a horizontal metaphor of the infinite and represent a total feeling of solitude.[44]

The story's heavy reliance on visual imagery and dramatic episodes can be explained by the fact that García Márquez originally wrote it as a film script. The following summary of the film's contents provides a valuable insight into the process of intertextuality:

> Brilliantly directed in Mexico by Brazilian Ruy Guerra and starring Irene Pappas as the monstrous grandmother, Claudia Ohana as Eréndira, and Michel Lonsdale as Ulises, the film captures visually some of the images García Márquez makes us conjure up in our minds. Particularly striking is the episode of the enamored Ulises changing the color of glass he touches. The shots of the desert and the sea point to their similarities, as Ulises had explained. The wind is absolutely pervasive. Onésimo Sánchez's phoniness is emphasized by his election poster in the film, reading "Onésimo es distinto" (Onésimo is different). According to Eréndira, that slogan backfires, for people know exactly what to expect from the politicians they are used to, who are all alike. (McNerney, 129–30)

Like most of the tales in this collection, "Innocent Eréndira" has an open ending. The episodic action provides a series of carnivalesque sequences followed by a dramatic departure of Eréndira into the unknown. Since the "slightest trace of her misfortune" was never found, it is clear that Ulises's slaying of the "white whale" provides him with nothing, while allowing Eréndira to escape. If the novella is judged as a commentary on exploitation and power, its worth can be clearly established, and it becomes a fitting preview of the author's most cogent study of power, *The Autumn of the Patriarch*.

The *Innocent Eréndira* volume no longer requires the annihilation of a created fictional world, as was the case in *One Hundred Years of Solitude*; instead, the finality is achieved by leaving the ends open (Janes, 87). We do not know where Eréndira or the man with wings goes, Janes states; nor do we know what becomes of Esteban's village, the ghost ship in Cartagena's harbor, or Mr. Herbert. We do know that Blacamán, in his own words, believes he will live forever, while Senator Onésimo Sánchez dies in a rage, knowing that he will lose Laura Farina. Still, the endings of these seven stories "confirm the fictitiousness of all endings save one but suggest with a chastened hopefulness the continuing, transforming power of ideas" (Janes, 87). Michael Palencia-Roth correctly concludes that the stories in this volume exorcise the earlier fiction of Macondo, giving the writer the opportunity to transform the Caribbean setting of these tales into a different Caribbean ambience in *The Autumn of the Patriarch*.[45] They serve as stylistic exercises and allow García Márquez to explore new themes and techniques in his later fiction.

Conclusion

Had Gabriel García Márquez never written a single novel, he would still merit an important niche in the history of Spanish American belles lettres. Some of his short stories have been judged the best examples of the genre ever written in Spanish America.[46] His writing career began with three short stories that appeared in Bogotá's *El Espectador* in 1947 and early 1948. When the political violence of 1948 forced him to return to the Caribbean coast, he entered the field of journalism but continued to write short fiction. In these early works the same themes he still cultivates today are evident: abject solitude in both a physical and a spiritual sense, the inexplicable intrusion of irrational forces in human life, and enduring skepticism of science and technology. Many of his early stories contain fantastic and imaginative episodes and show an early devotion to William Faulkner, Ernest Hemingway, and, to a lesser degree, Virginia Woolf. The invention of Macondo slowly emerges in this early fiction, as does his ability to fictionalize the reader of his literary creations.

By the mid-1950s García Márquez had established his reputation in both fiction and journalism, and in 1962, published the eight short stories of *Big Mama's Funeral*. This collection is important as a transitional work in which humor and hyperbole assume a prominent place. At the same time, concern for human dignity and the plight of the poor are primordial interests. These stories focus on individuals in a crumbling, violent society and on their efforts to confront the social reality surrounding them. In the title story of the collection the creation of myth is important as an anticipation of his later fiction. Macondo now exists in its definitive form, and the use of reappearing characters and episodes suggests the existence of a complete fictional universe. *Big Mama's Funeral* contains García Márquez's favorite short story, "Tuesday Siesta," a tale replete with technical stratagems learned from Hemingway.

Innocent Eréndira represents the work of a mature artist, with its magical realism, abundant humor, occasional optimism, and celebration of the power of human imagination. Although all of these eight stories resist conclusive critical exegesis, the writer is motivated here by a desire to entertain his fictionalized readers. Two of the tales were allegedly written for children, but all of them are accessible to readers of any age. All of these stories have an open ending, suggesting thereby the continuing, transforming power of the reader's own interpretations and ideas.

Two pieces of short fiction, originally published in *El Espectador* in 1981 and 1982, appeared in a single volume in Bogotá with the title *El rastro de tu sangre en la nieve; El verano feliz de la señora Forbes* (The trail of your blood in the snow; Mrs. Forbes's happy summer). Both deal with the experience of Colombians living in Europe. The former is the tale of the playboy Billy Sánchez de Avila and his bride, the beautiful Nena Daconte. Their honeymoon in Europe ends in tragedy when French doctors are unable to stop the flow of blood from the bride's ring finger. The latter story, recently released as a film with the title *The Summer of Mrs. Forbes*, recounts the experiences of two young boys, sons of a writer from the Caribbean, and their German governess, Mrs. Forbes. It is set on the island of Pantelaria off the southern coast of Sicily. By day Mrs. Forbes is an intransigent governess whom the boys attempt to poison. Their plan seems to be successful when they return to the villa and find it surrounded by police and a crowd of onlookers. But when the body is removed, it contains 27 deep knife wounds, apparently the result of a passionate episode in a secret part of her life not known by her employers. Although these two tales do not develop the themes García Márquez used in other works of fiction written during the early 1980s, they do recall the years he lived in Europe with his family, and the second story suggests an autobiographical element in its use of two sons of a Caribbean writer and their Mediterranean adventure.

Since 1972 García Márquez has devoted his time to the writing of novels. *The Autumn of the Patriarch* appeared in 1975, followed by *Crónica de una muerte anunciada* (*Chronicle of a Death Foretold*) in 1981. This second novel was published simultaneously in Barcelona, Buenos Aires, Mexico City, and Bogotá, and on the day of issue bookstores in this last city were forced to remain open until 10:00 P.M. to accommodate the eager crowds. *Love in the Time of Cholera* came out in 1985 with simultaneous editions in the same four cities. It was the June 1988 selection of the Book-of-the-Month Club in the United States and remained on the best-seller list of the *New York Times* for many weeks.

In March 1989 simultaneous editions of his most recent novel, *El general en su laberinto* (*The General in His Labyrinth*), appeared on three continents. Like *Love in the Time of Cholera*, it explores the abject solitude of old age, and through the use of flashbacks recounts the euphoria of victory and the solitude of defeat during the career of the Liberator, Simón Bolívar.

Recently García Márquez has devoted much of his time to the art of filmmaking, recalling his first journalism assignment as a film critic in the early 1950s. During 1955 he studied at the Experimental Center for the Cinema in Rome, and years later he lectured at the film school of the National University in Mexico City. Since 1985 he has been closely involved with the Foundation for the New Latin American Film, serving as its president and working with the institute it sponsors near Havana, Cuba, for aspiring Latin American filmmakers. Between 1987 and 1989 he simultaneously wrote six film scripts based on some of his short fiction and on two of his recent novels. The series, called *Amores difíciles* (Dangerous loves), was shown in August and September 1989 at the Festival Latino in New York and on Spanish television to raise money for the Cuban film institute. In August of the same year he directed a workshop for 10 Hispanic screenwriters at Robert Redford's Sundance Institute in Utah.

In the concluding paragraph of his 1982 Nobel address García Márquez makes reference to William Faulkner and to the enduring theme of solitude in his own work:

> On a day like today, my master William Faulkner said in this very place, "I refuse to admit the end of mankind." I should not feel myself worthy of standing where he once stood were I not fully conscious that, for the first time in the history of humanity, the colossal disaster which he refused to recognize thirty-two years ago is now simply a scientific possibility. Face to face with a reality that overwhelms us, one which over man's perceptions of time must have seemed a utopia, tellers of tales who, like me, are capable of believing anything, feel entitled to believe that it is not yet too late to undertake the creation of a minor utopia: a new and limitless utopia for life wherein no one can decide for others how they are to die, where love really can be true and happiness possible, where the lineal generations of one hundred years of solitude will have at last and for ever a second chance on earth.[47]

Part 1

This compelling appraisal of all his writing puts before the eyes of the world his fear that humanity may indeed destroy itself someday, and that writers like him, in their lonely solitude, have the obligation to create a just utopian world where those condemned to a hundred years of solitude will indeed have a second chance.

Notes to Part 1

1. Gabriel García Márquez and Mario Vargas Llosa, *La novela en América Latina: Diálogo* (Lima: Carlos Milla Batres, 1968), 8; hereafter cited in text.

2. For additional details concerning this period, see chapter 4 of Plinio Apuleyo Mendoza, *The Fragrance of Guava* (London: Verso Editions, 1983), 39–45; hereafter cited in text.

3. This information was provided to me in an interview with Gabriel Eligio García, father of the writer, in Cartagena on 11 March 1977. See Harley D. Oberhelman, "Gabriel Eligio García habla de Gabito," *Hispania* 61 (September 1978): 541–42. In the same interview his father asserted that the writer was born on 6 March 1927, not 1928 as most references state. The 1927 date is further confirmed in an article by Fernando Cortés in the 16 December 1985 issue of *Cromos* (no. 3544); the article records the certification of a parish priest in the baptismal book of Aracataca that Gabriel José, born on 6 March 1927, was baptized by him (p. 68).

4. Robert N. Pierce, "Fact or Fiction? The Developmental Journalism of Gabriel García Márquez," *Journal of Popular Culture,* 22, no. 1 (Summer 1988): 69; hereafter cited in text.

5. This and subsequent selected excerpts are from *The Collected Stories of Gabriel García Márquez* (New York: Harper & Row, 1984), 5; hereafter cited in text as *CS*.

6. Mario Vargas Llosa, "A Morbid Prehistory (The Early Stories)," *Books Abroad* 43 (Summer 1973): 454; hereafter cited in text.

7. Raymond L. Williams, *Gabriel García Márquez* (Boston: Twayne, 1984), 18; hereafter cited in text.

8. Robert L. Sims, "Narrating Violence and the Permutable Violence of Narration: The Evolution of Focalization in the Work of Gabriel García Márquez from 1947 to 1981," *Hispanic Journal* 10, no. 1 (Fall 1988): 54; hereafter cited in text.

9. See "El viaje de Ramiro de la Espriella," *El Universal,* 28 July 1949, 4. During this period García Márquez was living with the family of a friend, Ramón de la Espriella. When his friend left Cartagena in 1949, García Márquez commented in his "Punto y aparte" column of *El Universal* that Espriella, especially his contributions to the heated debates over Faulkner, would be sorely missed.

10. *Ojos de perro azul* (Rosario, Argentina: Equiseditorial, 1972). In the same year an unauthorized collection of nine short stories appeared under the

title *El negro que hizo esperar a los ángeles* (The black man who made the angels wait) (Montevideo: Ediciones Alfil, 1972). It contained the same short stories found in the first volume except for "La noche de los alcaravanes" and "Monólogo de Isabel viendo llover en Macondo," which were omitted.

11. See "Auto-crítica," *El espectador*, 30 March 1952, 16, 23.

12. According to superstition in the Caribbean coastal region of Colombia, curlews, also known as whimbrels or Hudsonian curlews, are able to tell time with their song and can likewise sense death. They reputedly peck out the eyes of anyone who imitates their song, as happened in the story.

13. For a complete and well-documented review of the years García Márquez spent in Cartagena and Barranquilla, see Jacques Gilard's *Obra periodística: Textos costeños*, vol. 1 (Barcelona: Bruguera, 1981), 7–56.

14. Donald McGrady, "Acerca de una colección desconocida de relatos por Gabriel García Márquez," *Thesaurus* 27, no. 2 (May–August 1972): 293–320; hereafter cited in text. This study also appears in Peter Earle, ed., *Gabriel García Márquez* (Madrid: Taurus, 1981), 60–80.

15. Jacques Gilard, "Cronología de los primeros textos literarios de García Márquez (1947–1955)," *Revista de crítica literaria latinoamericana* 2, no. 3 (1976): 103; hereafter cited in text.

16. Frank Dauster, "The Short Stories of García Márquez," *Books Abroad* 43 (Summer 1973): 467.

17. Claudia Dreifus, "Gabriel García Márquez Interview," *Playboy*, 2 February 1983, 172; hereafter cited in text.

18. Edith Grossman, "The Truth Is Stranger than Fact," *Review* 30 (September–December 1981): 72.

19. Gabriel García Márquez, *The Story of a Shipwrecked Sailor* (New York: Knopf, 1986), viii; hereafter cited in text as *Sailor*.

20. Luis Harss and Barbara Dohmann, *Into the Mainstream* (New York: Harper & Row, 1967), 314; hereafter cited in text.

21. Kathleen McNerney, *Understanding Gabriel García Márquez* (Columbia: University of South Carolina Press, 1989), 110; hereafter cited in text.

22. George R. McMurray, *Gabriel García Márquez* (New York: Ungar, 1977), 52; hereafter cited in text.

23. Susan Mott Linker, "Myth and Legend in Two Prodigious Tales of García Márquez," *Hispanic Journal* 9, no. 1 (Fall 1987): 93; hereafter cited in text.

24. Beth Miller, "Alegoría e ideología en 'La prodigiosa tarde de Baltazar': El artista del Tercer Mundo y su producto," *Revista de crítica literaria latinoamericana* 11, no. 23 (1986): 57; hereafter cited in text.

25. An excellent overview of the period known as *la violencia* can be found in Cida S. Chase, "'La Violencia' and Political Violence in García Márquez's Short Fiction," *Journal of Popular Culture* 22, no. 1 (Summer 1988): 73–82.

26. Melvin S. Arrington, Jr., "'La viuda de Montiel': Un retrato en miniatura de Macondo," in *En el punto de mira: Gabriel García Márquez*, ed. Ana María Hernández de López (Madrid: Pliegos, 1985), 67–68.

27. Enrique Sacerio-Garí, "Las flores de Borges en García Márquez," *Hispania* 70, no. 1 (March 1987): 64. For another study of this short story, see J. C. Mendizábal, "Ceguera clarividente en 'Rosas artificiales' de Gabriel García Márquez," *Káñina* 4, no. 1 (January–June 1980): 77–80.

28. See David William Foster, "The Double Inscription of the *Narrataire* in 'Los funerales de la Mamá Grande,'" in *Critical Essays on Gabriel García Márquez*, ed. George R. McMurray (Boston: G. K. Hall, 1987), 102–13; hereafter cited in text.

29. Shortly after the conquest of the New World, the Spanish crown rewarded the conquistadores with grants of land and Indians to work the land. This legal instrument was known as an *encomienda* and was the forerunner of the huge landed estates in the hands of single families still commonly found in parts of Spanish America.

30. Roger M. Peel, "The Short Stories of Gabriel García Márquez," *Studies in Short Fiction* 8, no. 1 (Winter 1971): 166; hereafter cited in text.

31. Judith Goetzinger, "The Emergence of a Folk Myth in 'Los funerales de la Mamá Grande,'" *Revista de Estudios Hispánicos* 6, no. 2 (May 1972): 243; hereafter cited in text.

32. Robert Sims, "The Creation of Myth in García Márquez' 'Los funerales de la Mamá Grande,'" *Hispania* 61, no. 1 (March 1978): 22.

33. Regina Janes, *Gabriel García Márquez: Revolutions in Wonderland* (Columbia and London: University of Missouri Press, 1981), 71; hereafter cited in text.

34. Mark Millington, "Aspects of Narrative Structure in *The Incredible and Sad Story of the Innocent Eréndira and Her Heartless Grandmother*," in *Gabriel García Márquez: New Readings*, ed. Bernard McGuirk and Richard Cardwell (Cambridge: Cambridge University Press, 1987), 117; hereafter cited in text.

35. Jorge Yviricu, "Transposición y subversión en 'Un señor muy viejo con unas alas enormes,'" in *From Dante to García Márquez*, ed. Gene H. Bell-Villada (Williamstown, Mass.: Williams College, 1987), 388.

36. Robert Coover, "The Master's Voice," *American Review* 26 (November 1977): 381.

37. Mary E. Davis, "The Voyage beyond the Map: 'El ahogado más hermoso del mundo,'" in *Critical Essays on Gabriel García Márquez*, ed. George R. McMurray (Boston: G. K. Hall, 1987), 160; hereafter cited in text. This essay is especially informative in its explanation of the relationship between Esteban and both classical and pre-Columbian myths. See especially pp. 164–67.

38. A helpful study of the relationship between the short story and Quevedo's sonnet can be found in Lidia Neghme Echeverría, "La ironía trágica en un relato de García Márquez," *Eco* 16 (October 1974): 627–46.

39. Rei Berroa, "Sobre 'Muerte constante más allá del amor,'" *Discurso Literario*, 1, no. 1 (Fall 1983): 8.

40. For a complete study of the problems of time in this short story see Germán Darío Carrillo, *La narrativa de Gabriel García Márquez* (Madrid: Ediciones de Arte y Bibliofilia, 1975): 139–59; hereafter cited in text.

41. See Mario Vargas Llosa, *García Márquez: Historia de un deicidio* (Barcelona: Barral Editores, 1971), 628.

42. Arnold M. Penuel, "The Theme of Colonialism in García Márquez' 'La increíble y triste historia de la cándida Eréndira y de su abuela desalmada,'" *Hispanic Journal* 10, no. 1 (Fall 1988): 68; hereafter cited in text.

43. See Joel Hancock, "Gabriel García Márquez's 'Eréndira' and the Brothers Grimm," in *Critical Essays on Gabriel García Márquez*, ed. George R. McMurray (Boston: G. K. Hall, 1987): 152–59.

44. Fernando Burgos, "Hacia el centro de la imaginación: *La increíble y triste historia de la cándida Eréndira y de su abuela desalmada*," *INTI: Revista de Literatura Hispánica* 16–17 (1982–83): 79–80.

45. Michael Palencia-Roth, "Entre dos mundos: La cuentística de García Márquez (1968–1972)," *Acta Litteraria Academiae Scientiarum Hungaricae* 27, no. 1–2 (1985): 96.

46. Gene H. Bell-Villada, *García Márquez: The Man and His Work* (Chapel Hill: University of North Carolina Press, 1990), 119. Of special interest is the chapter entitled "The Master of Short Forms," pp. 119–38.

47. Gabriel García Márquez, "The Solitude of Latin America: Nobel Address, 1982," trans. Richard Cardwell, in *Gabriel García Márquez: New Readings*, ed. Bernard McGuirk and Richard Cardwell (Cambridge: Cambridge University Press, 1987), 211.

Part 2

THE WRITER

Introduction

Over the years many critics have interviewed Gabriel García Márquez about his methods, his ideas, and his purpose in writing. The most extensive interview was conducted by his close friend Plinio Apuleyo Mendoza and translated into English as *The Fragrance of Guava*. Excerpts from this signal work appear as the first selection in this section. Another important interview was conducted by Claudia Dreifus for *Playboy*. This interview served to introduce the Colombian writer to a wide variety of readers in the United States. Rita Guibert's interview, published in *Seven Voices: Seven Latin American Writers Talk to Rita Guibert*, describes his life as a professional writer and explores other writers who have influenced him. Many of the ideas introduced in the Guibert interview are more extensively defined in Marlise Simons's *New York Times Book Review* interview published in 1982. Finally, a 1971 interview first published in Caracas in *Revista Nacional de Cultura* defines a theory of literature that has served him well for more than four decades.

Excerpts from *The Fragrance of Guava*
Plinio Apuleyo Mendoza and Gabriel García Márquez

His Craft

I began writing quite by chance, perhaps only to prove to a friend that my generation was capable of producing writers. After that I fell into the trap of writing for pleasure and then into the next trap of discovering there was nothing in the world I loved more than writing.

You've said writing is a pleasure. You've also said it is pure suffering. Which is it?

Both are true. At the beginning, when I was learning my craft, I wrote jubilantly, almost irresponsibly. I remember, in those days, I could easily write four, five, even ten pages of a book after I'd finished work on the newspaper around two or three in the morning. Once, I wrote a whole short story at a single sitting. . . .

What is your point of departure for a book?

A visual image. For other writers, I think, a book is born out of an idea, a concept. I always start with an image. *Tuesday Siesta*, which I consider my best short story, grew out of seeing a woman and young girl dressed in black with a black umbrella walking through a deserted town in the scorching sun. In *Leaf Storm*, it's an old man taking his grandson to a funeral. The point of departure for *Nobody Writes to the Colonel* was the image of a man waiting for a launch in the market-place in Barranquilla. He was waiting with a kind of silent anxiety. Years later in Paris I found myself waiting for a letter—a money order probably— with the same anxiety and I identified with the memory of that man. . . .

Let's talk now about the craft side involved in being a writer. Can you tell me who's been the greatest help to you in your long apprenticeship?

My grandmother, first and foremost. She used to tell me about the most atrocious things without turning a hair, as if it was something

From *Fragrance of Guava* by Plinio Apuleyo Mendoza and Gabriel García Márquez, trans. Ann Wright (London: Verso, 1983), 25–26, 30–36, 46–52, 59. © 1983 by Verso Editions. Reprinted by permission of Verso Editions.

she'd just seen. I realized that it was her impassive manner and her wealth of images that made her stories so credible. I wrote *One Hundred Years of Solitude* using my grandmother's method.

Was it through your grandmother that you discovered you were going to be a writer?

No, it was through Kafka, who recounted things in German the same way my grandmother used to. When I read *Metamorphosis*, at seventeen, I realized I could be a writer. When I saw how Gregor Samsa could wake up one morning transformed into a gigantic beetle, I said to myself, "I didn't know you could do this, but if you can, I'm certainly interested in writing." . . .

You loathe fantasy. Why?

Because I believe the imagination is just an instrument for producing reality and that the source of creation is always, in the last instance, reality. Fantasy, in the sense of pure and simple Walt-Disney-style invention without any basis in reality is the most loathsome thing of all. I remember once when I was interested in writing a book of children's stories, I sent you a draft of "The Sea of Lost Time." With your usual frankness you said you didn't like it. You thought the problem lay in your not being keen on fantasy and the argument devastated me because children don't like fantasy either. What they do like is imagination. The difference between the one and the other is the same as between a human being and a ventriloquist's dummy. . . .

Has journalism helped you at all in your literary profession?

Yes, but not, as is sometimes said, by teaching a more effective use of language. Journalism taught me ways of lending my stories authenticity. Draping Remedios the Beautiful in sheets (white sheets) for her ascent to heaven or giving Father Nicanor Reina a cup of chocolate (chocolate rather than any other drink) before he levitated six inches off the ground—these are really journalistic tricks, and very useful too. . . .

What do you think inspiration is? Does it exist?

It's a word which has been discredited by the Romantics. I don't see it as a state of grace nor as a breath from heaven but as the moment when, by tenacity and control, you are at one with your theme. When you want to write something, a kind of reciprocal tension is established between you and the theme, so you spur the theme on and the theme spurs you on too. There comes a moment when all obstacles fade away, all conflict disappears, things you never dreamt of occur to you and, at that moment, there is absolutely nothing in the world better than writing. That is what I would call inspiration.

Do you sometimes lose this state of grace during the course of a book?

Yes, and then I start thinking it out from the beginning again. These are the moments when I get a screwdriver and fix all the locks and plugs in the house or paint the doors green, because manual labor sometimes helps overcome the fear of reality. . . .

The way you treat reality in your books, especially in One Hundred Years of Solitude *and in* The Autumn of the Patriarch, *has been called "magical realism." I have the feeling your European readers are usually aware of the magic in your stories but fail to see the reality behind it. . . .*

This is surely because their rationalism prevents them seeing that reality isn't limited to the price of tomatoes and eggs. Everyday life in Latin America proves that reality is full of the most extraordinary things. To make this point I usually cite the case of the American explorer F. W. Up de Graff who made an incredible journey through the Amazon jungle at the end of the last century and saw, among other things, a river with boiling water, and a place where the sound of the human voice brought on torrential rain. In Comodoro Rivadavia, in the extreme south of Argentina, winds from the South Pole swept a whole circus away and the next day fishermen caught the bodies of lions and giraffes in their nets. In *Big Mama's Funeral* I tell the story of an unimaginable, impossible journey by the Pope to a Colombian village. I remember describing the President who welcomed him as bald and stocky so as not to make him look like the President in power at the time, who was tall and bony. Eleven years after this story was written, the Pope did go to Colombia and the President who welcomed him was bald and stocky just like the one in the story. After I'd written *One Hundred Years of Solitude*, a boy turned up in Barranquilla claiming to have a pig's tail. You only have to open the newspapers to see that extraordinary things happen to us every day. I know very ordinary people who've read *One Hundred Years of Solitude* carefully and with a lot of pleasure, but with no surprise at all because, when all is said and done, I'm telling them nothing that hasn't happened in their own lives.

So everything you put in your books is based on real life?

There's not a single line in my novels which is not based on reality.

Readings and Influences

I must warn you that the books I like are not necessarily the ones I think are the best. I like them for various reasons not always easy to explain.

You always mention Oedipus Rex *by Sophocles.*

Oedipus Rex, Amadis of Gaul, Lazarillo de Tormes, Daniel Defoe's *A Journal of the Plague Year,* Pigafetta's *First Voyage Around the World.*

And Tarzan of the Apes *as well.*

Yes, by Burroughs.

And the authors you return to most often?

Conrad, Saint-Exupéry.

Why Conrad and Saint-Exupéry?

The only reason you go back and read an author again is because you like him. Well, what I like about Conrad and Saint-Exupéry is the one and only thing they have in common—a peculiar way of approaching reality which makes it seem poetic even when it may be quite mundane.

And Tolstoy?

I never keep anything of his, but I do believe the best novel ever written is *War and Peace.*

But none of the critics have found any trace of these authors in your books.

I've actually always tried hard not to be like anybody else. I've always tried to escape from the authors I like rather than imitate them. . . .

[*Where is the influence of Virginia Woolf in your work?*]

I would be quite a different author from the one I am today if I hadn't read this passage from *Mrs. Dalloway* when I was twenty. "But there could be no doubt that greatness was passing, hidden, down Bond Street, removed only by a hand's-breadth from ordinary people who might now, for the first time and last, be within speaking distance of the majesty of England, of the enduring symbol of the state which will be known to curious antiquaries, sifting through the ruins of time, when London is a grass-grown path and all those hurrying along this Wednesday morning are but bones with a few wedding rings mixed up in their dust and the gold stoppings of innumerable decayed teeth." I remember reading this sentence as I sat swatting mosquitoes and dying of heat in a seedy hotel room, during that period when I was selling encyclopedias and medical books. . . .

Why did it make such an impression on you?

Because it completely transformed my sense of time. I saw in a flash the whole process of decomposition of Macondo and its final destiny. I wonder if it's not also the distant origin of *The Autumn of the Patriarch*, which is a book about the enigma of power, its solitude and its squalor.

Your list of influences must surely be much fuller than this. Whom have we left out?

Sophocles, Rimbaud, Kafka, Spanish Golden Age Poetry, chamber music from Schumann to Bartok.

Should we add something of Greene and a few drops of Hemingway? I remember seeing you reading them both very carefully when you were young. One of your stories, Tuesday Siesta *(your best, so you say) owes a lot to Hemingway's* A Canary for One.

Graham Greene and Hemingway both taught me purely technical tricks. Though I've always recognized their importance, they are surface values. I believe a real influence, an important influence, is when an author's work affects you so profoundly it alters some of your ideas about the world and about life in general.

Coming back to these profound influences, or rather the secret ones. Poetry? Did you perhaps want to be a poet when you were young, though you'll never admit it? . . . Even if you do recognize your literary education was primarily poetic.

I got interested in literature through poetry. Through bad poetry, popular poetry, the kind printed on calendars or sold as broadsheets. I found I like the poetry as much as I loathed the grammar in the Castilian texts which I did for my secondary school certificate. I loved the Spanish Romantics—Núñez de Arce, Espronceda.

Where did you read them?

In Zipaquirá. You know it as that gloomy town, six hundred miles from the sea, where Aureliano Segundo went to fetch Fernanda del Carpio. My literary education began at a secondary school there, where I was a boarder. I would read bad poetry on the one hand, and Marxist texts lent to me secretly by my history teacher, on the other. I would spend Sundays in the school library to stave off boredom. So, I began with bad poetry before discovering the good. Rimbaud, Valéry . . .

Neruda . . .

Neruda, of course. I consider him the greatest poet of the twentieth century, in any language. Even when he got into tight corners—with his political poetry, his war poetry—the poetry itself was always first-rate. I've said it before, Neruda was a kind of King Midas, everything he touched turned to poetry. . . .

Let's go on to your extra-literary influences. Other influences, which have been decisive in your work. Your grandmother, for instance.

I've already mentioned that she was a superstitious woman with a vivid imagination who terrorized me, night after night, with her stories from beyond the grave.

And your grandfather?

When I was eight he described episodes of all the wars he'd fought in to me. There's a lot of him in all my most important masculine characters.

Your grandparents actually represent a much wider and more profound influence—I mean that of the Caribbean coast of Colombia where you were born. There's obviously a superb oral narrative tradition there. You find the same tradition in song as well, in the "Vallenatos."[1] In fact, everyone there knows how to tell stories. Your mother, Doña Luisa, for example. I remember her telling us about a "comadre" of hers who took a walk in the garden every night, combing her hair. Naturally she'd been dead for ten years . . . but she still went on walking round the garden. Where does this ability to tell such extraordinary, such . . . magical tales come from?

My grandparents were of Galician origin and many of the supernatural things they told me about came from Galicia. However, I think this taste for the supernatural also comes to us through our African heritage. The Caribbean coast of Colombia is, together with Brazil, the part of Latin America closest to Africa. In this connection, the trip I made round Angola in 1978 gave me one of my most fascinating experiences ever. It was a watershed in my life. I expected to find a strange, totally unfamiliar world but from the moment I set foot in Africa and breathed in its air, I suddenly found myself back in the world of my childhood. Yes, I rediscovered my childhood there, the customs, all the things I'd forgotten. I even started having my child-hood nightmares again.

Part 2

In Latin America they teach us that we're Spaniards. It's partly true of course, since the Spanish ingredient is an undeniably important part of our cultural make-up; but on that trip to Angola I discovered that we're Africans as well or, rather, that we're a racial mixture. Our culture is enriched by contributions from many different races. I'd never been conscious of this before.

There are forms of culture with African roots in the Caribbean, where I was born, very different from those of the Altiplano where the indigenous cultures were strong. The exuberant imagination of African slaves, mixed with that of the pre-Columbian natives and added to the Andalusian taste for fantasy and the Galician cult of the supernatural, had produced an ability to see reality in a certain magical way. This is common to both the Caribbean and Brazil. Out of this has grown a literature, a music, a style of painting (like the Cuban Wilfredo Lam) which are the aesthetic expression of that region.

So the strongest influence on you, stronger than anything in your literary background, comes from your cultural and geographical identity. From the Caribbean. It is your world, the world you express. How does this influence come over in your books?

The Caribbean taught me to look at reality in a different way, to accept the supernatural as part of our everyday life. The Caribbean is a distinctive world whose first work of magical literature was *The Diary of Christopher Columbus*, a book which tells of fabulous plants and mythological societies. The history of the Caribbean is full of magic—a magic brought by black slaves from Africa but also by Swedish, Dutch and English pirates who thought nothing of setting up an Opera House in New Orleans or filling women's teeth with diamonds. Nowhere in the world do you find the racial mixture and the contrasts which you find in the Caribbean. I know all its islands: their honey-coloured mulattas with green eyes and golden handkerchiefs round their heads: their half-caste Indo-Chinese who do laundry and sell amulets; their green-skinned Asians who leave their ivory stalls to shit in the middle of the street; on one hand their scorched, dusty towns with houses which collapse in cyclones and on the other skyscrapers of smoked glass and an ocean of seven colours. Well, if I start talking about the Caribbean there's no stopping me. Not only is it the world which taught me to write, it's the only place where I really feel at home. . . .

I want the world to be socialist and I believe that sooner or later it will be. However, I have a great many reservations about what came in Latin America to be called "committed literature," or more precisely the novel of social protest (the high point of this literature). This is mainly because I think its limited view of the world and life does not help achieve anything in political terms. Far from accelerating any process of raising consciousness, it actually slows it down. Latin Americans expect more from a novel than an *exposé* of the oppression and injustice they know all too well. Many of my militant friends who so often feel the need to dictate to writers what they should or should not write are, unconsciously perhaps, taking a reactionary stance inasmuch as they are imposing restrictions on creative freedom. I believe a novel about love is as valid as any other. When it comes down to it, the writer's duty—his revolutionary duty if you like—is to write well.

Note

1. "Vallenatos" is a reference to music coming originally from the region around the town of Valledupar. It has a one-two rhythm, and the songs are improvisations based on legend, popular poetry, or current events. They now are popular throughout the coastal region.

Interview, 1983

Claudia Dreifus

Playboy: [L]et's pursue this question of literature and politics a bit further. You *are* fascinated by the relationship between the two subjects, aren't you?

García Márquez: ⸰ I'm fascinated by the relationship between literature and *journalism*. I began my career as a journalist in Colombia, and a reporter is something I've never stopped being. When I'm not working on fiction, I'm running around the world, practicing my craft as a reporter. . . . I have, as a result of the success of my novels, this huge reputation—and, yes, I am a Latin American, and considering all that is going on in Latin America, it would be a crime not to be interested in politics. If I came from a part of the world that didn't have Latin America's enormous political, economic and social problems, I could ignore politics. . . .

Playboy: In one of your short stories, "The Incredible and Sad Tale of Innocent Eréndira and Her Heartless Grandmother," a young prostitute tells her lover, "What I like about you is the serious way you make up nonsense." Is that Gabriel García Márquez talking about himself?

García Márquez: Yes, that is an absolutely autobiographical statement. It is not only a definition of my work, it is a definition of my *character*. I detest solemnness, and I am capable of saying the most atrocious things, the most fantastic things, with a completely straight face. This is a talent I inherited from my grandmother—my mother's mother—*Doña* Tranquilina. She was a fabulous storyteller who told wild tales of the supernatural with a most solemn expression on her face. As I was growing up, I often wondered whether or not her stories were truthful. Usually, I tended to believe her because of her serious, deadpan facial expression. Now, as a writer, I do the same thing: I say

Excerpted from "The *Playboy* Interview: Gabriel García Márquez," *Playboy*, February 1983, 65–77, 172–78. © 1982 by *Playboy*. Reprinted by permission. All rights reserved.

extraordinary things in a serious tone. It's possible to get away with *anything* as long as you make it believable. That is something my grand-mother taught me.

Playboy: [L]et's begin by asking you how much of your fiction has a basis in real life.

García Márquez: Every single line . . . in all my books, has a starting point in reality. I provide a magnifying glass so readers can understand reality better. Let me give you an example. In the "Eréndira" story, again, I have the character Ulises make glass change color every time he touches it. Now, that can't be true. But so much has already been said about love that I had to find a new way of saying that this boy is in love. So I have the colors of the glass change, and I have his mother say, "Those things happen only because of love. . . . Who is it?" Mine is just another way of saying the same thing that has always been said about love: how it upsets life, how it upsets everything.

Playboy: Over the past 20 years, we've seen an explosion of magic-realist novels from Latin America. What is it about the Latin world that encourages writers to work in this wild mixture of the real and the surreal?

García Márquez: Clearly, the Latin-American environment is mar-velous. Particularly the Caribbean. I happen to come from the Carib-bean part of Colombia, which is a fantastic place—completely different from the Andean part, the highlands.

During the colonial period of Colombian history, all the people who considered themselves respectable went to the interior—to Bogotá. On the coast, all that were left were bandits—bandits in the good sense—and dancers, adventurers, people full of gaiety. The coastal people were descendants of pirates and smugglers, with a mixture of black slaves. To grow up in such an environment is to have fantastic resources for poetry. Also, in the Caribbean, we are capable of believing any-thing, because we have the influences of all those different cultures, mixed in with Catholicism and our own local beliefs. I think that gives us an openmindedness to look beyond apparent reality. As a child growing up in the Caribbean village of Aracataca, I heard wonderful stories of people who were able to move chairs by simply looking at them. . . .

Playboy: How did the idea come to you to create Macondo out of the memories of Aracataca?

García Márquez: [W]hen I was a very young man—perhaps 20 years old, I tried to write a novel about the Buendía family titled *La casa* (The house). . . . I felt I was not yet ready to write a book as big as that. What I decided to do was start something easier and progressively learn how to write. Mostly, I wrote short stories. Around that time, when I was about 21, my mother asked me to take a trip with her to Aracataca—and that visit had a decisive impact on my career as a writer. You see, at that point, I was living in Barranquilla, a Caribbean city not far from Aracataca. My grandparents had both died, and my mother wanted to sell their house.

At first, I was very happy with the idea of returning to Aracataca. But when we got there, I was staggered. The town had not changed at all. I had the sensation that I had left time, that what had separated me from the town was not distance but *time*. So I walked along the streets with my mother and I realized that she was going through something similar. . . . I had the feeling that the whole town was dead— even those who were alive. I remembered everyone as they had been before, and now they were dead. That day, I realized that all the short stories I had written to that point were simply intellectual elaborations, nothing to do with my reality. When I returned to Barranquilla, I immediately sat down and wrote my first novel [*Leaf Storm*], which takes place in Macondo. Incidentally, on that trip, my mother and I passed a banana plantation that I had often seen as a child. There was a sign on the place; it was called Macondo. . . .

Playboy: [Y]ou wrote, "Literature was the best plaything that had ever been invented to make fun of people." Do you think that's true? . . .

García Márquez: There is a definite state of mind that exists when one is writing that is called inspiration. But that state of mind is not a divine whisper, as the romantics thought. What it is, is the perfect correspondence between you and the subject you're working on. When that happens, everything starts to flow by itself. That is the greatest joy one can have, the best moment. I am never better and my house is never better and my relations with everybody are never better than when a book is turning out well.

Excerpts from *Seven Voices: Seven Latin American Writers Talk to Rita Guibert*

Rita Guibert

When García Márquez came to New York in 1971 to receive an honorary degree from Columbia University, Rita Guibert was granted a three-hour interview with the writer in the Plaza Hotel. In their extensive conversation a great deal of information concerning his theories of literature and work habits were revealed. Excerpts from this interview follow.

Could you describe what the life of a professional writer is like?

Listen, I'll tell you what a typical day is like. I always wake very early, at about six in the morning. I read the paper in bed, get up, drink my coffee while I listen to music on the radio, and at about nine . . . I sit down to write. I write without any sort of interruption until half past two. . . . I haven't answered the telephone all morning . . . my wife has been filtering calls. We lunch between half past two and three. If I've been to bed late the night before I have a siesta until four in the afternoon. From that time until six I read and listen to music—I always listen to music, except when I'm writing because I attend to it more than to what I'm writing. Then I go out and have coffee with someone I have a date with and in the evening friends always come to the house. Well . . . that seems to be an ideal state of things for a professional writer, the culmination of all he's been aiming at. But, as you find out once you get there, it's sterile. I realized that I'd become involved in a completely sterile existence—absolutely the opposite of the life I led when I was a reporter. . . . Yes, there's a natural tendency—when you have solved a series of material problems—to become bourgeois and shut yourself in an ivory tower, but I have an urge, and also an instinct, to escape from that situation—a sort

From *Seven Voices: Seven Latin American Writers Talk to Rita Guibert*, by Rita Guibert (New York: Alfred A. Knopf, 1973), 311–12, 314, 318, 323, 326–27, 335–37. Reprinted with permission of the author.

of tug-of-war is going on inside me. Even in Barranquilla [where he began his secondary school] I realize that I'm losing sight of a large area that interests me, out of my tendency to confine myself to a small group of friends. But this isn't me, it's imposed by the medium, and I must defend myself.

I think the theme of solitude is a predominant one in your work.

It's the only subject I've written about, from my first book until the one I'm working on now [in 1971], which is an apotheosis of the theme of solitude. Of absolute power, which I consider must be total solitude. I've been writing about that process from the first. . . . I think the critics who most nearly hit the mark were those who concluded that the whole disaster of Macondo—which is a telluric disaster as well—comes from this lack of solidarity—the solitude which results when everyone is acting for himself alone. That's a political concept, and interests me as such—to give solitude the political connotation I believe it should have.

[Do] you prefer the spoken word to writing?

Of course. The splendid thing is to tell a story and for that story to die there and then. What I should find ideal would be to tell you the story . . . I'm now writing, and I'm sure it would produce the same effect I'm trying to get by writing it, but without so much effort. At home, at any time of day, I recount my dreams, what has happened to me or not happened to me. I don't tell my children make-believe stories, but about things that have happened and they like that very much. Vargas Llosa . . . takes my work as an example and says I'm a seedbed of anecdotes. To be liked because I've told a good story, that's my true ambition. . . . The type of recognition I have always desired and appreciated is that of people who read me and talk to me about my books, not with admiration or enthusiasm, but with affection.

[Your stories] all begin with an old man. . . .

The guardian angel of my infancy was an old man—my grandfather. My parents didn't bring me up, they left me in my grandparents' house. My grandmother used to tell me stories and my grandfather took me to see things. Those were the circumstances in which my world was constructed. And now I'm aware that I always see the image of my grandfather showing me things.

What influences have you been conscious of?

The notion of influence is a problem for the critics. I'm not very clear about it, I don't know exactly what they mean by it. I think the fundamental influence on my writing has been Kafka's *Metamorphosis*, although I don't know whether the critics who analyse my work discover any direct influence in the books themselves. I remember the moment when I bought the book, and how as I read it I began to long to write. My first stories date from that time—about 1946, when I had just gotten my baccalaureate. . . . [Kafka] made me want to write. A decisive influence, which is perhaps more obvious, is *Oedipus Rex*. It's a perfect structure, wherein the investigator discovers that he is himself the assassin . . . an apotheosis of technical perfection. All the critics have mentioned Faulkner's influence. I accept that, but not in the sense they think when they see me as an author who read Faulkner, assimilated him, was impressed by him and, consciously or unconsciously, tries to write like him. That is more or less, roughly, what I understand by an influence. I was born in Aracataca, the banana-growing country where the United Fruit Company was established. It was in this region, where the fruit company was building towns and hospitals and draining some zones, that I grew up and received my first impressions. Then, many years later, I read Faulkner and found that his whole world—the world of the southern United States which he writes about—was very like my world, that it was created by the same people. And also, when later I traveled in the southern states, I found evidence—on those hot, dusty roads, with the same vegetation, trees, and great houses—of the similarity between our two worlds. One mustn't forget that Faulkner is in a way a Latin American writer. His world is that of the Gulf of Mexico. What I found in him was affinities between our experiences, which were not as different as might appear at first sight. Well, this sort of influence of course exists, but it's very different from what the critics pointed out.

"A Talk with Gabriel García Márquez"

Marlise Simons

García Márquez explained his preoccupation with what to say at the 1982 Nobel award ceremony in the following terms: ". . . I must try and break through the clichés about Latin America. Superpowers and other outsiders have fought over us for centuries in ways that have nothing to do with our problems. In reality we are all alone." [He later gave his Nobel speech the title "The Solitude of Latin America."]

In response to the idea that he writes intuitively, García Márquez stated: ". . . The whole notion that I am an intuitive is a myth I have created myself. I worked my way through literature, reading, writing, reading and writing—it's the only way. I learned a lot from James Joyce and Erskine Caldwell and of course from Hemingway. But the tricks you need to transform something which appears fantastic, unbelievable into something plausible, credible, those I learned from journalism. The key is to tell it straight. It is done by reporters and by country folk."

His difficulties with the United States State Department and his political views were summarized in this fashion: "There is no way one can relate to contemporary cultural life without going to the United States. Ironically that is the place with the most serious students and the best analyses of my work. Yet the State Department plays this game with me in which I may or may not be able to go there. . . . If I were not a Latin American maybe I wouldn't [be a political activist]. But underdevelopment is total, integral, it affects every part of our lives. The problems of our societies are mainly political. And the commitment of a writer is with the reality of all of society, not just with a small part of it. If not, he is as bad as the politicians who disregard a large part of our reality. That is why authors, painters, writers in Latin America get politically involved. I am surprised by the little resonance authors have in the United States and in Europe. Politics is made there

From the *New York Times Book Review*, 5 December 1982, 1, 18–19. © 1982 by the New York Times Company. Reprinted by permission.

78

only by the politicians. The era of Sartre and Camus has definitely passed."

He concluded with an assessment of the role of journalism in his career: "I have always been pulled by the world of journalism. And I am still fascinated by the relationship between journalism and literature."

"Conversations with Gabriel García Márquez"

Armando Durán

In response to a question about the problem of the treatment of reality in fiction, García Márquez made the following comments: "The only thing I know without any doubt is that reality is not limited only to the price of tomatoes. Daily life, especially in Latin America, undertakes the task of proving this. . . . It is enough to read the papers, and open one's eyes, in order to feel willing to shout along with the French college students: 'Power to the imagination.' Remember that the great majority of things in this world, from spoons to heart transplants, were in man's imagination before becoming reality. Socialism was in Karl Marx's imagination before being in the Soviet Union. These cliché truths lead to poetry, for they authorize us to believe that perhaps the earth is not round, but rather began being so when many men, for the comfort of the period, imagined it to be that way. I believe that this system of exploration of reality, without rationalist prejudices, opens up . . . a splendid perspective. And it should not be believed that it is an escapist method: sooner or later, reality ends by agreeing with imagination."

Excerpted from *Review 70* 3 (1971): 115–17. Published by the Center for Inter-American Relations, New York. Originally published in Caracas in *Revista Nacional de Cultura* 29:185 (July–September 1968): 23–34.

Part 3

THE CRITICS

Introduction

Since the publication of *One Hundred Years of Solitude* in 1967, and especially since García Márquez won the Nobel Prize in 1982, an abundance of critical commentary concerning his fiction has been produced throughout the Western world. Included in this section is Raymond L. Williams's "The Writer as Journalist," a careful analysis of the literary themes evident in García Márquez's early journalism, themes that later came to dominate his short fiction and novels. Regina Janes's "Learning a Craft" considers the early short stories as a prelude to the more mature writings published after 1961. "The Precursors: Short Novels and Stories," by Kathleen McNerney, is a perceptive reading of the author's early short fiction, as well as a study of the stories contained in the 1962 edition of *Big Mama's Funeral*, without a doubt the most significant monument to his early efforts in the field of short fiction. Finally, there is the signal contribution of Mark Millington, "Aspects of Narrative Structure in *The Incredible and Sad Story of the Innocent Eréndira and her Heartless Grandmother*." Here Millington offers the arrival-carnivalization-departure formula as a basic frame of reference for all the tales in this collection.

Raymond L. Williams

Journalism has been a constant presence in García Márquez's literary and personal biography. It was journalism, in the early years in Cartagena and Barranquilla, that provided him with the opportunity to earn a living with the pen. As has been suggested in the discussion of "A Tale of a Castaway," journalism was essential to the development of García Márquez's fiction. . . . García Márquez has stated that "journalism helped maintain contact with reality, which is essential to literature."[1]

García Márquez the novelist has gained far more from journalism than just "contact with reality." There were crucial initial lessons in writing for the general public—and the related fictionalization of a reader. Certain techniques considered basic to journalism have become constant in García Márquez's fiction: the creation of a high level of interest from the very first lines of a text; the use of journalistic details.

García Márquez also maintains that he became a good journalist by reading literature.[2] The broad range of fictional styles and techniques with which he became acquainted during the early years on the coast undoubtedly afforded new possibilities for his journalism. A reading of his journalistic writings during this period, in fact, shows a writer experimenting with a variety of styles, techniques, and genres. Both the enormous volume of García Márquez's journalism and its intimate relationship to his fiction make his journalistic writings essential to a complete study of his work. . . .

García Márquez's career in journalism stretches from the late 1940s to the present, although there have been unproductive periods, usually when he has been preoccupied exclusively with writing fiction. In the context of this total career as a novelist, the most interesting period of journalism was his preprofessional days as a novelist, from the late

Excerpted from *Gabriel García Márquez* by Raymond L. Williams (Boston: Twayne Publishers, 1984), 134, 140–54. © 1984 G. K. Hall & Co. Reprinted by permission of Twayne Publishers, a division of G. K. Hall & Co.

1940s to the mid-1950s. The journalism of these years, compiled in a volume entitled *Textos costeños*, will be the central focus of the remainder of this [study].

The journalistic pieces which García Márquez published from 1948 to 1952 would be of interest even if they did not happen to become the first writings of a Nobel Prize winning author. They are a fascinating review of the period, including regular commentary on such persons as President Truman, the films of the times, and the advent of the hydrogen bomb. They provide a sense of daily life in Colombia—many cultural and political events of no lasting value—and a sense of the times as seen from Colombia. They often carry the fresh stamp of innocence, the mark of a twenty-year-old writer who is writing before public postures or pretense became important.

During this period he published over four hundred short pieces, on a wide variety of topics and in several genres. Exact classification of all this writing in traditional genre definitions would be extremely difficult and probably pointless, but the articles range from political commentary to fiction. They include notes that might be called "social commentary"—not necessarily social criticism, but observations concerning local, national, and world events. This social commentary is the most common content of García Márquez's column. Some of the journalism is cultural or literary commentary. Again, "commentary" is more appropriate than a term such as "literary criticism"; the publication of a new book more often elicited praise of the author and affirmation of friendship with this fine person than an attempt at objective review of the book. A considerable portion of García Márquez's total journalistic production is fiction. This writing includes short stories, short fictional anecdotes, and even short sections of fiction intended to become a novel. This type of writing sometimes eludes categorization: a news item which the journalist received over the teletype could be converted into an anecdote with a substantial portion of fiction and artistic transformation.

Affinities to the later fiction and direct origins of it are present in this journalism. In some pieces the similarities are reflected in a distantly comparable idea or vaguely reminiscent tone. Some themes are the direct origins of García Márquez's central preoccupations in his later novelistic career. The investigative scholar of García Márquez will find these writings rich material: such pieces as an overt attempt at imitating Kafka, his praise of Faulkner, and short "Notes for a Novel" (with characters from the later Macondo) are definitive proof of much of what has been speculated on the basis of interviews and analysis of García Márquez's later fiction. . . .

Some of the articles relate directly to the short stories published later. An incident mentioned with reference to the Mississippi River relates so directly to the story "The Last Voyage of the Ghost Ship" that this article could well be the initial catalyst for the later creation of the story. In this article, published in April 1951, García Márquez mentions having heard the story of a "ghost ship" ("barco fantasma") on the Mississippi. This empty ship floated along the Mississippi with its lights out. Like the ghost ship in "The Last Voyage of the Ghost Ship," this ship seems to have supernatural powers: "con la rueda lateral girando en virtud de una fuerza sobrenatural" (638).[3]

One humorous incident in "The Handsomest Drowned Man in the World" is the naming of the drowned man. He is named when one of the inhabitants suddenly declares: "He has the face of someone named Esteban." García Márquez wrote an article in February 1952 dealing with naming. This piece, entitled "Hay que parecerse al nombre" ("One Must Be Like the Name"), is devoted to the matter of the relationship between a person's name and this person's physical traits. The article begins with the author recalling having heard a remark quite similar to the naming of Esteban in "The Handsomest Drowned Man in the World": "Tenía cara de llamarse Roberto, pero se llamaba José" ("He had the face of someone named Roberto, but his name was José," 716).

The link between Kafka and García Márquez's early fiction can be made direct with a reading of these articles. The most interesting piece of writing in this context is a "Caricature of Kafka," a brief parody of Kafka's writing, published in August 1950. This piece contains several elements easily recognizable by the reader of Kafka: the characters are identified by letters rather than names; the protagonist has just completed a trip throughout the night; the environs are of cold steel and ugly modernity; the protagonist's effort in crossing a bridge is thwarted by an official who is a part of a vast hierarchy; the protagonist suffers from an initial indecision and ultimate failure.

Nightmares which relate directly to both García Márquez's initial stories and Kafka appear with some regularity in the early journalism. It is obvious that during this period García Márquez was fascinated with the subject of nightmares. One of his articles published in June 1950, entitled "Una parrafada" (A paragraph), refers to "pesadillas kafkianas" ("Kafkaesque nightmares"). It is only a passing remark in the context of an article which communicates one of his rare moments of boredom with everyday life and writing and perhaps even a little frustration with the routines. The following month, July 1950, he published a brief fictional anecdote titled "Pesadillas" (Nightmares) whose central focus is nightmares. In this story a man enters a newspaper office and offers his nightmares to the director. The entire story is the dialogue between the two men, with the visitor attempting to convince the director of the value of publishing his dreams in the newspaper. It is a particularly notable story when one takes into account García Márquez's attempts at creating an "other reality" in his short stories published during the 1948–52 period. . . . Another fictional anecdote published later the same year (October 1950), entitled "Un professional de la pesadilla" (A Nightmare Professional), deals with a character who is a nightmare specialist. This man, Nathaniel, spends twenty years concentrating on having the best nightmares possible. He purposely induces indigestion and nervousness in order to produce the strangest and most "difficult" nightmares. The story describes his numerous techniques and the exotic nightmares they produce.

Much of the journalism published during this period does not necessarily relate to the later fiction in such a direct fashion as the type of articles cited above. Rather, this journalism shares themes that have a regular presence in his fiction. A reading of the journalism confirms that García Márquez has been constantly preoccupied with such themes as death, the rational and the nonrational, the effects of modern science and technology, the common man, and insanity. . . .

A perusal of García Márquez's early journalism is fascinating for several reasons. Foremost of these is the opportunity it affords the reader of his later, truly professional fiction to observe the developments of García Márquez's interests, themes, and narrative techniques. The basic attitudes and world view of the twenty-year-old journalist are amazingly consistent with those of the forty- and fifty-year-old novelist and spokesman for Latin-American intellectuals. The later journalism, logically enough, is similar to both the journalistic writing and certain aspects of the fiction. Neither space nor the relative importance of this journalism within the context of García Márquez's total writing career allows a complete review of this considerable body of writing in its entirety.

A brief review of the journalism written a few years later, after the stay in Europe, shows a writer more concerned with international issues than before. A volume later edited under the title *Cuando era feliz e indocumentado* (When I was happy and undocumented) is a collection of this journalism published originally in 1958 in Caracas. These articles are witness of a García Márquez impressively knowledgeable about world affairs in general, from the intricacies of Venezuelan politics to the current situation in Cuba and Senegal.

The raucous "El año más famoso del mundo" (The most famous year of the world) is an entertaining overview of world events of the year 1957. He covers the major events in Europe, the United States, Asia, and Latin America. The imaginative juxtaposition of the typical political front-page news with human-interest stories both deflates standard news-story-type journalism and makes for a supremely humorous annual review. He subtitles one section, for example, "Gromyko Moves Up and Brigette Bardot's Neckline Goes Down." He gives the two events equal importance in his report of the year's important events; in fact, he explains Bardot's news first. Similarly, to the news of the Soviet Union's new long-range missile, García Márquez adds the news that the West, more interested in the imminent birth of Gina Lollabrigida's firstborn, paid little notice to the Soviet military gestures. The piece functions on the basis of this constant juxtaposition of the standard political news of supposed major significance with the very human and often equally trivial. García Márquez understands well what most people read with interest most of the time in newspapers.

The remainder of this volume contains pieces much more serious and newslike in tone and context, and others that are much more like fiction. One article, for example, is a report on the present policies with Italian immigrants, and another about a local bishop's work to distribute wealth more equally in Venezuela. A report on the process of obtaining medicine for a dying rabies victim features the best narrative techniques of the suspense thriller. A report on the political situation in Colombia concludes with the perspective of that person who always enjoys a privileged position in García Márquez's writing, the common man in the street.

In recent years García Márquez has published journalism regularly. During the late 1970s and early 1980s he wrote a weekly column for *El Espectador,* the Colombian newspaper that originally sent him to Europe in the mid-1950s as a correspondent. His syndicated columns also appear regularly in much of the Hispanic world. Some of his political positions set forth in these articles, such as his support for Fidel

Castro's government in Cuba and his criticism of the policies of the United States, have become more unequivocally delineated than they were before. They are articles covering a broad range of topics that any reader can recognize as having been penned by a master of both standard journalism and innovative fiction.

Notes

1. See Edith Grossman, "The Truth Is Stronger Than Fact," *Review* 30 (September–December 1981): 71–73.
2. Ibid., 72.
3. *Textos costeños*, with prologue by Jacques Gilard (Barcelona: Bruguera, 1981). Further quotations from García Márquez's journalism are from this volume.

Regina Janes

García Márquez published his first short story in 1947 at the age of nineteen; nineteen years later, he was finishing the novel that would make him rich and famous or documented and unhappy, if we are to believe the title he gave in 1974 to a collection of early reportage. In the course of that apprenticeship, he happened on many techniques to which he would later return, invented characters and places he would later develop more fully, and discovered the distinctive manner he would henceforward deploy for the fictional treatment of political issues—a wide-eyed, deceptively guileless wonder at the scenes he has invented and the brutality of which men are capable. Alternating between material essentially personal and material political and social, he adopted in succession a variety of authors as models, abandoning each in turn, until he found the tone that, in *One Hundred Years of Solitude*, would unify and transform personal memories and political convictions. . . .

Excerpted from *Gabriel García Márquez: Revolutions in Wonderland* by Regina Janes (Columbia: University of Missouri Press, 1989), 16–25, 29. © 1981 by the Curators of the University of Missouri. Reprinted by permission of the University of Missouri Press.

As García Márquez changed his narrative point of view, he also altered the way in which he managed the impossible or the marvelous,
moving from impossible premises in the earliest stories ("The Third
Resignation," "Eva Is inside Her Cat," "Night of the Curlews,"
"Someone Has Been Disarranging These Roses") through the natural-
ization of the impossible as dream or hallucination ("Eyes of a Blue
Dog," "Nabo, the Black Man Who Made the Angels Wait," "One Day
after Saturday," "Monologue of Isabel Watching It Rain in Macondo")
to the marvelous real proper, the rhetorical heightening of events de-
cidedly odd, but not impossible ("Balthazar's Marvelous Afternoon,"
"Montiel's Widow," and "One Day after Saturday" again). . . .

Dividing these early fictions into "personal" material and "sociopolitical" material had perhaps best be left to the author's promised mem-
oirs, but in interviews and through Vargas Llosa, he has provided
enough biographical information to make it clear that by the late 1950s
the personal had disappeared into the sociopolitical and that the two
kinds of material, readily distinguished in the earlier fictions, had now
become inextricable. The political transformation of the colonel-grand-
father figure between *Leafstorm* and *No One Writes to the Colonel* is familiar and transparent enough, but a more interesting case appears in
the maternal line in the treatment of García Márquez's grandmother
in "Bitterness for Three Sleepwalkers" and of his mother and himself
in "Tuesday Siesta." "Bitterness for Three Sleepwalkers" treats the
ambivalent responses of the adult children of a family to the senile
decay of their mother. Using an ill-defined "we" as narrator, García
Márquez makes his family-narrator appear radically unsympathetic because the responses they articulate to the situation are so inadequate
to it. "She," the mother, appears a prisoner, an object, until, in a sudden shift, "we" express a last, pathetic wish that a girl child be born
in the house so that "we" could believe "she" had been born renewed.
The biographical germ of this story seems to have been the decay of
García Márquez's own grandmother in his parents' house, repeated in
Ursula in *One Hundred Years of Solitude,* and the peculiar narrative technique seems to have been a means of coping with a certain ambiguity
of feeling, expressing simultaneously the author's complicated dislike
of such degeneration and his dislike of his own dislike. "Tuesday Siesta," on the other hand, is a brief and stringent celebration of the
stoicism and courage of a woman of the people and her daughter in the
face of economic deprivation and the violent death of an only son and

brother, the support of the family. It requires no biographical information to make its events or tone comprehensible, and the only mystery that surrounds it is why, good as it is, García Márquez should say that this is his favorite among all his short stories. That preference may derive from the biographical origin of this story in the momentous trip the author made with his mother to Aracataca to sell his grandmother's house. He was not a girl, he was well over twelve years old, and no one had been shot breaking into a widow's house; but the return to Aracataca and the house in which he had been raised, so different in memory from its present reality, provided the story's central situation of unbearable isolation under a blazing sun and aroused in García Márquez the desire to write the story of the decayed house and town that would become *Leafstorm* and later *One Hundred Years of Solitude*. But crucial as this event was to García Márquez as man and as author, it has disappeared altogether into another story with its own clear and unambiguous political, social, and human purpose.

Of the earliest stories, Vargas Llosa has said that their problem is the lack of a story, and he attributes that lack to the very young artist's repudiation of his own immediate experience as subject, which forced him to fall back on his reading, in this case Kafka. These storyless stories also refuse, deliberately, to specify the usual components of stories: time, setting, character, names, relationships between characters. But no writer can evade his own experience altogether, not even a would-be Kafka, and García Márquez rejected his external biographical experience, whether as a child, adolescent, or young man, in favor of a symbolization of internal experience that comments on the quality instead of the events of that experience. To this preference of symbolic over self-regarding autobiographical representation, we owe the distinctive achievement of the later fictions, but in the earliest tales the symbolization turns inward, rendering an idiosyncratic, private condition rather than setting up a reverberation in our common experience.

Of the first three stories, two are complementary explorations of solitude and powerlessness, familiar themes in García Márquez's later work, pursued through situations that will become images in the later work. In "The Third Resignation" the protagonist is a young man who died seventeen years earlier at the age of eight and has continued to grow in his coffin. The cessation of growth marked a second death but brought with it the sudden fear that he would now be buried alive. The third resignation is the third death, the acceptance of his powerlessness to protest his remission to the earth. "Eva Is inside Her Cat" inverts the terms of the first: instead of life, the heroine rids herself of her beauty; instead of being fixed in a coffin, she is everywhere and nowhere, a point of consciousness; instead of a mere seventeen years of death, she lives 3,000 years of dispersal; instead of accepting a final death on the other side of fear, she is awakened to a consciousness of time's passing by the surge of an ungratifiable desire for the taste of an orange. Obviously, such characters do not act in the world in relation to other characters but exist only in the mind, and in the mind only as it is aware of an abstract state, death or beauty, fear or desire. To render the psychological state of his characters, the author depends almost entirely on the characters' awareness of physiological sensations, reducing the mind to a neurological center, aware of the smell of violets or formaldehyde, the contractions of the viscera, or a hot prickling like ants crawling under the skin. Situation substitutes for action, physiology for emotion, and bodies for character. It is not a happy substitution, particularly when we consider that although a young man may feel that his life is a living death, no young woman has ever wished to rid herself of her beauty—complained of it, repined at it, pitied herself for it, yes! but willed it away, never. Time takes care of that for her, she knows. But in spite or perhaps because of this lapse with respect to the truths of feminine psychology, these bodily situations correspond to a profound sense of solitude and powerlessness. Solitude defines the characters' circumstances in the young man's inability to communicate with his mother when she measures him and in Eva's escape into atemporality from her beauty, insomnia, ancestors, and the memory of the dead boy in the ground. Powerlessness reaches to the body itself. Before we discover his moribund immobility, the hero of "The Third Resignation" suffers a painful noise in his head that he would like to grasp, fling away, and cannot. Eva can neither reconcile herself to her beauty nor find her cat to eat her orange. Solitude and powerlessness will remain the dominant polarities of García Márquez's fictions even when he is exploring that most powerful of figures, the eternal dictator, and in the later fictions corpses will appear beautiful, undecayed, and heavy; men will fear burial alive; beautiful young women will be oblivious to their beauty and disappear into the atmosphere; physiological sensations will be poeticized as icy fungi or lilies growing in the gut; but the characteristic tone will have been transformed. While solitude will remain irremediable, while characters will always be trapped in the decaying body and entangled by nostalgia, the later characters will have something to lose, some relationship, activity, or memory to which they grapple. But these characters have no system of locomotion: they are possessed of a fear of dying without a motive for living.

The twenty-year-old author seems to have recognized the problem, for slowly, very slowly, his characters begin to move. In "The Other Side of Death" our hero lies in bed, awake, alive, though his twin brother is dead in the ground and that is what is on his mind. By "Dialogue with the Mirror," he has found a job and has gotten up to shave in front of a mirror that reflects his movements before he makes them, as breakfast cooks in another room. And although "He must have thought—since no other state of mind occupied him—about the thick preoccupation of death" and, of course, his dead brother under the ground, the morning sun on the garden is drawing him "toward another life, which was more ordinary, more earthly, and perhaps less true than his fearsome interior existence."[1] In "Bitterness for Three Sleepwalkers" the restricted narrative "he" has become a barely identifiable "we," but there at last materializes a character separate from the central consciousness of the story in the aged, senile mother. The invention of a character and the determination to turn to a more ordinary existence served him well, for in "Eyes of a Blue Dog" our customary young man returns, but in relation to another character—he has found a woman, though they meet only in dreams and she will not let him touch her, in spite of undressing in front of him and in spite of searching for him hopelessly when she is awake. "Eyes of a blue dog" is the phrase that would let them find each other outside the dream, but within the dream, she knows that she remembers it waking and he does not, for "You're the only man who doesn't remember anything of what he's dreamed after he wakes up" (*CS*, 54). As that concluding sentence indicates, "Eyes of a Blue Dog" integrates dream and commonplace, catching what in real circumstances would be an unrealistic complaint and turning it into the reasonable complaint of a woman in unreasonable and well-defined circumstances. For, with one exception, from this story on García Márquez leaves behind the early vagueness that attempts to suggest great things by blurring outlines and solves the problem of plotlessness, as it must always be solved, by the invention of characters in conflict with one another.

The single exception is his first "political" story, "The Night of the Curlews" (1953), which reverts to the deliberate uncertainties of the stories prior to 1950 in an attempt, it seems, to intimate the powerlessness of the common people relative to the atrocities perpetrated by the powerful when their fellows will not believe what has happened to them, though it is reported in newspapers and visible on their bodies. Three nameless men, sitting in a courtyard, are blinded by curlews. No one will help them; no one believes their story, regarded as a newspaper trick to raise circulation. The child who identifies them as the men whose eyes were plucked out by curlews refuses to guide them home lest the other boys throw stones at him. Instead, he goes back to reading *Terry and the Pirates*, like the policeman in *In Evil Hour*. The men finally sit down in the sun, waiting for it to burn their faces before moving back to the wall. The curlews are explicated in *Leafstorm:* at the end of that novel, the boy remembers that Ada has told him that curlews sing when they smell a dead man, and the boy expects all the curlews to sing as the door is opened. One of the blinded men had been imitating the song of the curlews when they attacked. It is a claustrophobic little tale, the reader, like the characters, having lost "the notion of distance, time, direction" (*CS*, 88), the central event never described, the world reduced to walls and gropings, the resolution deliberately irresolute. Instead of rendering a highly particularized world within which symbolically significant or allusive events take place, the author has, in his first excursion into symbolic politics, tried to imitate the sensation of helplessness from the inside, from the point of view of the victims. The perpetrators remain unnamed and insignificant. In the terms of the story, no crime has been committed; there is only a failure of solidarity on the part of the townspeople. That failure parallels the response of Macondo to the banana massacre in *One Hundred Years of Solitude,* though the novel is more sympathetic to the terrorized town than is this story. But the townspeople here, as in *Leafstorm* and "Tuesday Siesta," are rendered with considerable hostility as potentially or actively malevolent, suggesting a profound change in García Márquez's attitude toward "the people" as he and his fictions became more determinedly political.

When García Márquez's first ten stories were pirated in the early 1970s under the title *Eyes of a Blue Dog,* he advised his readers not to read them, but if they must, to steal them from the bookstores. Since then, he has authorized their republication in his collected stories and their translation. That change of heart was probably economic, but it would be pleasant to think that, like the fondness he expressed for *Leafstorm* after *One Hundred Years of Solitude,* he recognized in them his first attempts to play various narrative tricks he would master in *The*

Autumn of the Patriarch and that he has forgiven them for being so je-
june. Except for "Isabel Watching It Rain in Macondo" (which had
been removed from *Leafstorm* and developed as a separate story),
"Nabo" is the only one of the early stories to have been translated and
republished with the author's permission before the appearance of *The
Autumn of the Patriarch*, after the publication of *One Hundred Years of
Solitude*. Earlier than "Isabel," it is also the only one of the early stories
to exploit all the devices appearing in these stories that would reappear
in *The Autumn of the Patriarch*. Like "The Other Side of Death,"
"Nabo" experiments with internal shifts in narrative point of view.
Like "Bitterness for Three Sleepwalkers," it adopts a communal "we"
for part of the narrative ("Bitterness for Three Sleepwalkers" uses the
communal "we" throughout). And it alone plays with the extended
sentence containing shifts in point of view and juxtapositions of different times.

But since "The Other Side of Death" is earlier than "Nabo" and is
distinctive in its experimentation with shifts in narrative point of view,
let us begin there, more especially since it provides a glimpse, perhaps,
of the origin and fate of the patriarch's double in *The Autumn of the
Patriarch*. The story begins in the restricted third person, but as the
nameless character begins to remember the dream from which he has
just awakened, a textbook surrealistic dream, he begins to comment
on it in the first person: "They were traveling in a train—I remember
it now–through a countryside—I've had this dream frequently—like a
still life, sown with false, artificial trees bearing fruit of razors, scissors,
and other diverse items—I remember now that I have to get my hair
cut—barbershop instruments. He'd had that dream a lot of times but
it had never produced that scare in him" (*CS*, 14). Later, as "he" begins to think about his dead twin in the ground, the resources of ty-
pography are called upon to effect an identification between the "him"
narrating and the "him" in the ground as he recalls his brother's death
throes: "Many hours had already passed since the moment in which *he
saw* [narrator] him twisting like a badly wounded dog under the sheets,
howling, biting out that last shout that filled his throat with salt, using
his nails to try to break the pain that was climbing up *him* [brother],
along his back, to the roots of the tumor. He couldn't forget *his*
[brother] thrashing like a dying animal, rebellious at the truth that had
stopped in front of *him* [ambiguous], that had clasped *his* [brother] body
with tenacity, with imperturbable constancy, something definitive, like
death itself" (*CS*, 17). In *The Autumn of the Patriarch*, this dead twin

will lose his own life in the patriarch's and will again die a terrible death in front of the survivor, but the narrative shifts will define character and relationships among characters and will impel the action onward. Here the shifts form part of a retreat from action: suddenly awakened, instead of getting up, our hero runs through his dream, remembers and identifies with his dying brother, and descends to the earth with him as he begins to wait for his own death. The movement outward, away, becomes a spiral that leads back into the self and ends in paralysis; but, while other people may wait for the patriarch to die, he himself will have none of it.

"Nabo" confines its shifts in point of view to an alternation between an omniscient narrator and a communal, familial "us" that first appears a third of the way through the story. As in "Bitterness for Three Sleepwalkers," the use of a communal voice serves to communicate hostility toward that voice by denying it affective responses in a story charged with pathos at other levels. The story turns on loss, on communication begun and broken between Nabo and the black man in the band who reappears as the hallucinated angel and, more importantly, between Nabo and the mute girl who learns to speak his name. But the communal voice has no share in that communication; "He was no longer delirious, but he kept on talking until they put a handkerchief in his mouth. . . . When we took out the handkerchief so that he could eat something, he turned toward the wall" (*CS*, 72).[2] In the first part of the story, the pathos implicit in Nabo's predicament is relieved by the comic nagging of the angel that he hurry up and join the choir. But as Nabo's relationship with the mute girl is developed, the uncomprehending, uncaring "we" appear to correct the pathos, to control and check it, suggesting the author's resolute resistance to sentiment, as the other relationships in the story suggest his strong impulse toward it. Given that the family in "Nabo" has fed and housed a mad former servant, now useless, for fifteen years, a considerable degree of art has gone into making the reader remember only that they gagged him and tied him down.

"Nabo" might also seem to anticipate *The Autumn of the Patriarch* in its temporal shifts, but its use of those shifts is closer to *Leafstorm* than to the later novel in that the different times are juxtaposed rather than entwined. The same absence of fluidity marks, but does not mar, the experimentation with the extended sentence in the story's final, one-sentence paragraph (thirty-nine lines in Spanish, forty-six in English). The sentence relates a continuous movement, Nabo's bursting out of his room, but its progress is interrupted momentarily by the insertion with dashes (parentheses in the translation) of different times and the thoughts of different characters. In its last third, however, when Nabo has reached the backyard without finding the stable, the sentence shifts brilliantly and smoothly back to the girl in the room who cries out his name. Though the technique will be carried much further in *The Autumn of the Patriach* and "The Last Voyage of the Ghost Ship," it serves in all three cases to reveal an exhibition of helpless power, to bind together endings and beginnings that contrast brutality and an epiphany, to evoke a moment, its history, and the response to that moment, all in a single syntactic unit, a headlong verbal act to contain a headlong physical act. . . .

[From the ponderous weight of Faulkner in "Nabo,"] García Már-quez transferred his stylistic allegiance to Hemingway, the master of effaced narration who had learned much about leaving things unsaid from the prolix master of the unspoken, Henry James. The change of style was accompanied by a change of subject matter, a more deliberate and explicit treatment of the social and political questions that had formed part of the milieu of *Leafstorm*, but were not in themselves objects of attention. In "Two or Three Things about the Novel of *La Violencia*" and "A Man Has Died a Natural Death" (on the occasion of Hemingway's suicide), García Márquez specified the elements in Hemingway that had made the greatest impression on him: the objec-tivity of his style, the experiential base of his subjects, the image of a fiction as an iceberg, in which the tenth above the surface, all that is visible to the eye, suggests the far greater mass below. In his fictions, the influence of Hemingway manifested itself in the abandonment of first-person (singular or plural) and restricted third-person narration for an omniscient but largely effaced narrator; in increasingly economical, specific, and significant description; and in spare but clear plotting that produces the "iceberg" effect.

Notes

1. Gabriel García Márquez, *Collected Stories* (New York: Harper & Row, 1984), 40. Further citations from this edition will appear in the text.

2. The English version of "Nabo" appears in *Leafstorm and Other Stories*, trans. Gregory Rabassa (New York: Harper & Row, 1972), 217.

Kathleen McNerney

Though any piece of writing done by García Márquez can stand on its own, certain common themes, characters, and situations make it useful to look at some of his short fiction, particularly the earlier stories, in relation to his three long novels and to each other, for García Márquez weaves familiar faces and places in and out of these works. This technique has been seen variously as puzzle pieces, episodes that seem to be seeds of other, more developed episodes, or miniatures. The Eréndira who passes so briefly through the pages on *One Hundred Years of Solitude*, for example, becomes the subject of the film and novella she entitles, complete with heartless grandmother and itinerant photographer. Far from being repetitious, the incidents are as intriguing as life. Just when we thought we knew the judge or the priest from one story, he appears in another, and we see a new aspect of his character which explains something that had gone before, as if people we know superficially one day were to tell us their deepest secrets. Like a detail in a photograph blown up many times, the enlargement shows us what was always there but didn't come to our attention before.

Thus, we meet in *Leaf Storm* the aged widow Rebeca, while the colonel who attends the ostracized doctor's funeral remembers that other famous colonel, Aureliano Buendía; his daughter Isabel tells us that her father and mother were first cousins. Still another colonel, the one to whom no one writes, also recalls Aureliano and the capitulation known as the Treaty of Neerlandia. Judge Arcadio, such a corrupt tyrant in *One Hundred Years of Solitude*, appears in *In Evil Hour* as more a friend of the bottle than anxious for power.

García Márquez's earliest stories, written when he was barely twenty and under the influence of his favorite writers, especially Woolf, Hemingway, and Faulkner, were published first in periodicals and finally gathered together under the title *Ojos de perro azul* (Eyes of a Blue

Excerpted from *Understanding Gabriel García Márquez* by Kathleen McNerney (Columbia: University of South Carolina Press, 1989), 98–100, 109–15. © 1989 University of South Carolina Press. Reprinted with permission.

Dog), the name of one of the stories. The title is characteristic in its bizarre flavor: the stories, for the most part, are excursions into realities and perceptions, and into irrational, surreal, and sometimes nightmarish states of consciousness. In the least successful stories technique becomes more important than content, as if the author were still a bit too self-conscious. Half the stories are an exploration of death: "The Third Resignation" examines the stages, or phases, of death, with many hints of the circular motion of time so perfected in *One Hundred Years of Solitude*. "The Other Side of Death" uses García Márquez's first set of twins in a grotesque look at death and finding one's identity. "Dialogue with a Mirror" repeats the doubling motif with an image reflected in a mirror which gains its own autonomy. The passage of time is mentioned abruptly in "Eva Is Inside Her Cat," a story in which beauty is seen as Eva's enemy, and in which her only contact with the realm of the senses is the desire to eat an orange. In the title story a man and woman who meet only in their dreams cannot remember those dreams upon waking. Perhaps the most Faulknerian of the tales in its atmosphere is "Nabo, the Black Man Who Made the Angels Wait." Nabo, having been kicked by a horse he was grooming, is locked up in the stable because of his resulting madness. His only possible communication is with the retarded girl he had taught how to use the phonograph. The most straightforward of the stories is probably "The Woman Who Came at Six O'Clock," in which a woman who always comes into the bar at six wants an alibi for what she has just done and convinces the barman to say she came at five-thirty that day.

The stories are replete with surprising images and startling cerebral voyages. Mirrors and reflections, doubling, smells and tastes, and a preoccupation with time and death are characteristic threads in these early experimental tales, threads which are to be picked up and fully developed in other works. . . .

The Stories in *Big Mama's Funeral*[1]

Perhaps the most striking image of dignity in García Márquez' work, however, is the figure of a woman. In the story that opens *Big Mama's Funeral*, which is also García Márquez's own favorite, "Tuesday Siesta," a woman and her daughter, both dressed in black, get off the train during the heat of the day and ask the priest for permission to visit the cemetery. At first the priest resists, because it is siesta time, but her quiet dignity prevails. In answer to the priest's queries, she states, with her head held high, that she wants to visit her son, who was shot last week for being a thief. The contrast between the ineffectual priest and the proud woman is at its peak when he pompously asks her whether she ever tried to get him on the right track:

> "He was a very good man."
> The priest looked first at the woman and then at the girl, and realized with a kind of pious amazement that they were not about to cry. The woman continued in the same tone:
> "I told him never to steal anything that anyone needed to eat, and he minded me" (*CS*, 105).

The author tells us that his stories often begin with a visual image rather than an idea. He mentions this story as an example, and it is indeed a convincing one. If his early stories were perhaps too metaphysical, the later collections show a certain influence of his growing interest and experience in film, and more success in capturing certain feelings and sensations. In "One of These Days" the overwhelming sensation is that of a toothache, set against the backdrop of the wars. It is an episode which appears in a somewhat different version in *In Evil Hour*. In the story the dentist is a courageous partisan on the wrong side. But the balance of power is shifted as a result of the mayor's devastating toothache. He orders the dentist to extract it or be shot. The dentist extracts it without anesthesia, with the words: "Now you'll pay for our twenty dead men" (*CS*, 109). The balance of power returns to its earlier status as the dentist sarcastically asks whether to send the bill to the town or to the mayor. "It's the same damn thing" (*CS*, 110) is the mayor's succinct, and accurate, reply. The war and civil repression are skillfully understated, or unstated, in the reaction of the child to the mayor's threat to shoot his father: he registers neither fear nor surprise, so accustomed is he to the violence of the status quo.

"There Are No Thieves in This Town" reminds the reader of Spanish literature of a story by nineteenth-century Valencian novelist Vicente Blasco Ibáñez, "El hallazgo" ("The Windfall"), in which a thief hurriedly grabs a pile of quilts from his victims' house, only to find an infant inside when he arrives at home.[2] His heart goes out to the child, and he returns it to the home, but by now it has gotten late and the family catches him. He goes to jail. The thief in García Márquez's story steals billiard balls, not a child, but he finds himself in a similar situation: what can he do with them? At first he hides them.

The whole town is talking about the theft, and a victim is found to blame. Since the townspeople don't want to believe it was one of them, they accuse a black man who is passing through. The thief still holds his tongue, but since the town's only recreation was the billiard table, he finally decides to return the balls. The owner accuses him of stealing money as well and takes him to the mayor, "not so much for being a thief as for being a fool" (*CS*, 137). The power of gossip, so central to *In Evil Hour,* is an interesting part of this story. When the thief and his wife go to find out what is being said in the town, they are almost convinced of the townspeople's version of the events, because the people tell what they heard with such conviction.

"Balthazar's Marvelous Afternoon" is the triumph of the nobility of a poor man over the meanness of a rich man, and at the same time of art over political power. Balthazar's beautiful cage, which needs no birds for it could sing by itself, was made with little Pepe Montiel in mind, and cannot be sold to anyone else, even when Pepe's father refuses to pay for it. José Montiel's anger at the construction of the cage for his son is heightened by Balthazar's generosity in giving it to Pepe. Balthazar can't bear the child's tantrum, whereas the father doesn't seem to be affected. José Montiel, however, perceives the gift as a threat to his authority and throws the carpenter out. That the cage had been constructed, that he had not been paid for it, and that he had left it behind do not seem important to Balthazar, until he goes to the bar and sees that the supposed sale is important for his peers, who are delighted at the thought of anyone extracting money from Montiel. Balthazar can't bear to let them down, so when they buy him a beer, he buys rounds for everyone. Since the carpenter is unused to the consumption of alcohol, the festivities excite his dream to build thousands of other cages, selling them all to rich people. His understanding of rich people, from what he has seen, is that they all have ugly and contentious wives, and that they are so unhealthy that they can't even get mad, and that they're all about to die, so he must hurry up with his plans to build cages to sell them. Dead drunk but still clinging to his dream at the end, he realizes that his shoes are being taken, but he doesn't want to break the spell of the happiest dream of his life.

But José Montiel does get mad, and dies from it. His widow is the only person in town in "Montiel's Widow" who believes he has died of natural causes. So hated is this usurper of people's land that everyone expected him to die from a bullet in the back. The story explores the widow's world of unreality, and how she benefits from his despotism without knowing what is going on. While Montiel murders his poor enemies and runs the rich ones out of town so he can steal their belongings, she sympathizes with the victims. She believes her husband has helped those who had to flee, and chastises him for helping them, since they won't remember him for it. Since her premise is wrong—that her husband helped them—her conclusion is wrong. They will certainly remember him. The usurped lands are in danger of being taken by others when Montiel is no longer around, but the widow is oblivious to everything, never having been in touch with reality. She urges her children to stay in Europe, and the only time she smiles is when she receives a letter from her daughter describing the pink pigs in the butcher shops of Paris: "At the end of the letter, a hand different from her daughter's had added, "Imagine! They put the biggest and prettiest carnation in the pig's ass" (*CS*, 153). She only wants to stop living. It is Big Mama, in whose house she lives, who tells her in a dream that she will die when the tiredness starts in her arm.

"One Day after Saturday" paints the elderly Father Antonio Isabel as a totally methodical man, always absorbed in the temptations of the senses and how to make sermons out of them, a man who connects the dead birds in the town, not with the record-breaking heat, but with the Apocalypse. He has never been able to persuade the equally aged widow Rebecca to reveal to him the mysterious circumstances of her husband's death years before. When Father Antonio Isabel takes a dying bird into her house, he seems to fear her concupiscence more than the suspicions that she is a murderer. The birds cause his Sunday sermon to turn to the appearance of the Wandering Jew, and when he collects money to fight off the terrible apparition, he gives it to the poor young man who was just arrived in the town, seeking his mother's pension. In his mind's wanderings he believes that maybe it is possible to be happy, if only it weren't so hot.

"Artificial Roses" shows the intergenerational tensions in a family as a result of repression and hypocrisy. The roses Mina makes and her false sleeves are as unreal as the appearances she must keep up. Her blind grandmother sees better than anyone into Mina's reality, but only to try to control her behavior. In a comment on madness, which García Márquez deals with in depth in *One Hundred Years of Solitude*, this story shows the lucid grandmother as crazy, but as she says herself, "Apparently you haven't thought of sending me to the madhouse so long as I don't start throwing stones" (*CS*, 183).

The title story in this collection, "Big Mama's Funeral," is the first example of an accumulation of hyperbole, a technique García Márquez uses extremely well here and in later works. An enumeration of Big Mama's properties and powers is endless and fanciful, including a brilliant collection of set phrases particularly from the field of journalism. When she dies, it hadn't occurred to anyone to think she was mortal. In a way she is the prototype of the patriarch to come, though her power is inherited from her family, and kept in part because she never married. Matriarch of everyone and "well enough endowed by Nature to suckle her whole issue all by herself, [she] was dying a virgin and childless" (*CS*, 189).

The narrator who tells the whole story in all its details sees his role as protector of the truth against distortions and memory loss, and he is anxious to do so before the historians get hold of it and before the garbage men sweep up the garbage from the funeral forever. This grand funeral is to be attended by the pope, for Big Mama died in the odor of sanctity.

When García Márquez wrote the story, a visit by the pope to Colombia was unthinkable, but even so he changed the physical appearance of the President of the Republic in order not to be accused of pointing to anyone in particular. But by the time the real pope came to Latin America, the President of the Republic fit the description in the story. Big Mama dies as a saint, or at least as much of a saint as the mother of the patriarch, Bendición Alvarado, whom he tries to have canonized. Both Bendición and Big Mama also come almost full circle chronologically, since they are presented after their deaths as young women again. In the case of Big Mama, a photograph of her when she was twenty-two and the printed word make her instantly famous even among those who had never seen her. Big Mama had been more powerful than even the government; her secret estate includes forged electoral certificates. A patriotic hero as well as a saint, she is given the honors due a soldier killed in battle. Big Mama had melted into her own legend.

Notes

1. References to this collection are found in Gabriel García Márquez, *Collected Stories* (New York: Harper & Row, 1984).

2. "The Windfall" appears in Ibáñez, *The Last Lion and Other Tales* (Boston: John W. Luce, 1919).

Mark Millington

I am going to begin with beginnings. Each story in *ISS*[1] begins with an arrival—a space or a consciousness is invaded by an unknown presence. But the nature of the invading presence differs: in "Constant Death" and "Blacamán" it is human (Onésimo Sánchez and Blacamán respectively); in "Very Old Man" it is part-human (the bird-man); in "Drowned Man" it was formerly human (Esteban's corpse); in "Sea" and "Incredible Story" it is a natural phenomenon (the smell of roses and a wind respectively);[2] and in "Last Journey" it is an object (the ghost ship). But in four of the stories the source of the invading presence is the same: in one way or another, the sea is associated with the arrival in "Very Old Man," "Sea," "Drowned Man" and "Last Journey," and in the first two of these the invading presence returns to the sea at the end. And in all of the stories the arrival has the same extraordinary effect—it becomes the focus of widespread, sometimes all-absorbing, attention—and in each case the arrival represents the inception of a series of events that will occupy the remainder of the story. The effect of the arrival is to disrupt—it introduces instability into a pre-existent situation, and that instability produces interest and also movement. The interest stimulated by the new arrival centres on a common reaction in several stories: the need to discover the meaning of the disruption. But the invading presence also seems to produce a release of energy in the characters and so to create a new pattern of life. In both respects the arrival is a beginning—a point of inception.

The fact that in certain stories the characters need to interpret the arrival, to establish the meaning of the invading presence, is a sign of the destabilizing character of the event. The diversity of the interpretations and the confusion felt is most graphically apparent in "Very Old

Excerpted from "Aspects of Narrative Structure in *The Incredible and Sad Story of the Innocent Eréndira and Her Heartless Grandmother*," in *Gabriel García Márquez: New Readings*, ed. Bernard McGuirk and Richard Cardwell (Cambridge: Cambridge University Press, 1987), 117–28. © 1987 by Cambridge University Press. Reprinted with the permission of Cambridge University Press.

Man." Here the desire to understand is powerful but the capacity to comprehend minimal: the bird-man is variously seen by the villagers as a nightmare, a shipwrecked sailor, an angel and a circus animal; and their confusion is shared by the chain of ecclesiastical interpreters extending up to the Vatican, which is notable for its failure to produce even a conjectural interpretation. The same overloading of interpretative skills is evident in "Drowned Man," where the desire to establish whether Esteban is human is simply swept aside by unquestioning awe in the face of his extraordinary beauty. In both of these cases (and in the other stories with inanimate invasions) the new arrival sets up no dialogue with the community that is invaded—the bird-man and Esteban simply arrive and are observed. They provide no self-explanation, and that accounts, in part, for the disputes that arise as to their nature and even existence (examples of the latter are in "Sea" and "Last Journey"). In each case, the interpretations are attempts to accommodate the unknown within everyday frames of knowledge. Given the nature of the new arrivals, the interpretations are not surprising, though they are certainly not definitive either. They also provide a valuable means of assessing the workings of characters' minds, that is, their capacity for rational thought, and this factor is crucial for the reader's response, in potentially stimulating an ironic view of characters.

More important than the question of characters' interpretations is the new direction that their lives take. The change results from the instability that the new arrivals produce, since characters are stimulated to undertake action, and action means change. It is not that any specific response is demanded, any inescapable action forced upon them, but that a field of possibility is opened up. In the case of "Blacamán" the arrival of Blacamán in the narrator's life effects a transformation: it means leaving home, trying to be a clairvoyant, fleeing from the U.S. marines, suffering at the hands of Blacamán and finally discovering his real gifts for healing the sick and resurrecting the dead, in other words, a multifarious field of new experience. In "Very Old Man" the bird-man's arrival involves Pelayo and Elisenda willy nilly in trying to cope with the sheer physical problem of crowds of onlookers, and that problem leads to their financial triumph, the building of a luxurious house and a new job for Pelayo: life is transformed. In "Last Journey" the strength of the general disbelief in the narrator's story about the ship provides the motive for his proving himself and achieving maturity[3]—the ship's intrusion (into his consciousness alone at first) stimulates his resourcefulness and leads him to act decisively. Again, a new direction is taken. Even in the less obvious case of "Constant Death," a similar structure of new movement is apparent. In this case, the point of view is partially with the new arrival, Onésimo Sánchez, whereas in most stories it is with those intruded upon; but there is also a prior intrusion into Sánchez's consciousness before the start of the story, namely the information that he is about to die. The conjunction of the two new "arrivals" is what counts, for Sánchez's presence in Rosal del Virrey brings contact with Laura, but the presence of the awareness of death stimulates him to act in a way that is largely contrary to his past behaviour. So the intruding presences again lead to particular forms of innovatory action.

The structure so far isolated, therefore, involves various kinds of invasion or arrival, which sometimes stimulate interpretation but which, above all, destabilize a pre-existent situation and lead to the inception of new movement, new courses of action. And the remarkable feature of the new movement in *ISS* is that the individuals involved, who first perceive the intruding presence, are frequently joined by the whole community—a broad expansion takes place, which makes the disequilibrium a shared and festive event. There is a multiplication of interest which often extends beyond the bounds of the local population. The fair motif is central to this expansion. In "Very Old Man" the bird-man's arrival initially affects only Pelayo and Elisenda, but overnight there is a large influx of people from the neighbourhood (pp. 12–13) and subsequently of huge crowds of people from far and wide who stretch in a line over the horizon waiting to see the prodigy (p. 15). This influx brings with it a variety of fairground performers from around the Caribbean who temporarily transform the community—life undergoes a process of carnivalization. A similar kind of response follows on the news of Esteban's arrival in "Drowned Man": "Some women who had gone to fetch flowers in the neighbouring towns returned with other women who didn't believe what they had been told, and these others went for more flowers when they saw the dead man, and they brought more and more, till there were so many flowers and so many people that it was almost impossible to walk" (p. 55). And likewise in "Sea" three outsiders go away and return with a great crowd of people who bring with them a variety of fairground acts and festivities; their arrival poses the same problems as in "Drowned Man": "The men and the woman who came to Catarino's store went away one Friday, but they came back on the Saturday with a crowd. More came on the Sunday. They swarmed everywhere, looking for something to eat and somewhere to sleep, till it was impossible to walk along the street" (p. 32).

These influxes are experienced from the standpoint of the places which are invaded, but a reverse perspective exists in "Blacamán" where the protagonists are the invading fairground performers. Indeed, "Blacamán" opens by exploiting and extending an archetypal fairground frame: Blacamán stands on a table selling a patent medicine and verbally and physically performs his way to success. The narrator joins him in his exploits and ultimately becomes a showman whom the crowds flock to see—the fair becomes a permanent way of life for him. "Constant Death" draws on the same frame; in this case, the fair or carnival is Sánchez's election campaign. The trappings of the campaign create the same fairground atmosphere as in Blacamán's performance. Standing on his platform, Sánchez presents his case to the people in a euphoric and histrionic verbal *tour de force*, while his helpers build an illusion of a secure future—in effect, a promise that carnival will take over permanently: [These phrases] were the formulas of his circus. While he spoke, his helpers threw into the air handfuls of small, paper birds, and the pretend animals took on life, fluttered over the wooden platform, and went away out to sea. At the same time, others took out of the wagons theatrical trees with felt leaves and set them up behind the crowd on the ground of saltpetre. Finally they put together a cardboard façade showing imitation redbrick houses with glass windows, and with it blocked from view the squalid slums of real life (p. 61). Nelson Farina's description (in French) makes the point about Blacamán's and Sánchez's similar techniques incisively: "Shit . . . he's the Blacamán of politics" (p. 63).

The same perspective is apparent in "Incredible Story": again the viewpoint is with the travelling performers—the carn(iv)al[4] entertainment provided by Eréndira—and again there is a process of expansion as Eréndira and her grandmother gain experience and money (they buy a circus tent, p. 134), and as they are joined by lottery-ticket sellers, a photographer, a band and foodstalls. Eventually their presence in a town seems to convert it into a single, huge brothel and gambling den; the queue waiting for Eréndira, ". . . comprising men of varied race and diverse condition, seemed like a snake with human vertebrae that was dozing across plots of land and squares, through many-coloured bazaars and noisy markets, and emerged from the streets of that deafening city of traders in transit. Every street was a public gambling house, every street a bar, every door a refuge for fugitives" (p. 145). The process of carnivalization and the capacity for extension could scarcely be more vivid.

This move into expansion and carnivalization amplifies the localized effects of new arrivals; it is a consistent structural motif throughout *ISS*, but there is no precise repetition of detail in each story; it is a general rhythm and developmental strategy.

It is appropriate to move from that general framework of development to the specifics of the structural relations between the events in the narrative thread. In some stories there is not a strong sense of necessary connection. It is clear that the narrative line may not depend on strict relations of causality. The sequence of narrated events can be fairly contingent, though chronological time *is* predominant. This is most noticeable in "Incredible Story" and "Sea," which are fairly episodic, and where the cause and effect relations between events are therefore rather weak. What narrative coherence there is may derive from other factors. In "Sea," especially, there are many discrete phases and minor sequences—either involving new situations, or new characters in repeated situations. Exemplifying the former are the multiple and somewhat haphazard facets of Sr. Herbert's "philanthropic" activities, and exemplifying the latter the different responses of Tobías and Petra to the arrival of the smell of roses. In addition, the lack of a constant protagonist in "Sea" reinforces the episodic quality. The story is dependent for coherence on the stability of time and place reference, and on two general situational contexts, which appear in succession in the story but have no causal connection: the response to the rose smell, and the revelries of the carnival.

"Incredible Story" lacks the coherence provided by a single setting, but it does have a fairly constant trio of protagonists. Even though the specifics of situation change rapidly from one section to the next, often with no causal link between them (sections six and seven being exceptions), there is an implicit, underlying problem that is constant: will Eréndira ever be free of her grandmother's tyranny? But this may come through as a clear, cohesive thread only at a late stage—it is not foregrounded until the end of section six—and that deferral contributes to the episodic character of the story. Similarly "Blacamán" has no tight narrative line—one episode is not linked closely to the next—and that is emphasized by the summarizing narration, in which a general description of events bypasses the specifics of sequential narrative.

Clearly the sheer demands of writing involve a certain line, one which reading inevitably retraces at a basic level of contact, but the episodic character of some stories is made yet more apparent by considering two other factors which, conventionally, provide cohesion. The first is that characters rarely have overt or identifiable goals or plans of actions—and there is no inner discourse or monologue to make any plain. (Again, the quality of characters' minds is made apparent negatively.) That particular absence is obvious in "Incredible Story," where, as I have suggested, the long-term problem, "Will Eréndira ever be free?," is clearly alluded to only near the end. "Last Journey" is remarkable as an exception, in that the narrator declares his basic aim in the first line and the whole story is built around showing how it is achieved. The second factor is the lack of any mystery or tension to resolve; this kind of element would provide a strong sense of direction and a high level of coherence, that is, coherence with clear relevance to the semantic core of a story, as against the second order coherence of time, place, and character. Mystery or tension might provide tighter relations in the narrative sequence, but there is little use of either.

Given that some of the stories do not rely heavily on strong causal links to sustain forward movement, it is interesting to consider how endings are achieved. If there is little causal emphasis, what relation can an ending have with what precedes it? Is there any evidence to suggest that the endings in *ISS* act as points of culmination or resolution? And, if not, how does each story create a "sense of an ending"? The key factor here is departure. Most of the stories rely on departures to provide a "sense of an ending," that is to create an impression that a "natural" cycle has been completed: the departure terminates what the arrival inaugurated, which is something that readers can accept by drawing on cultural knowledge and without needing an explanation of how or why it came about. "Very Old Man" ends with the growth of the bird-man's feathers which creates the possibility of flight and departure. The ending of "Sea" depends on departures too, implicit ones: the rose smell seems to vanish, Sr. Herbert bids farewell and the crowd of people which overwhelmed the town goes away also. But these departures are not culminations, they are no more than an indication that the carnival is over. Both "Constant Death" and "Incredible Story" end with deaths—that is, departures of a sort—but in neither case is it a culmination or resolution; in "Constant Death" the death of Sánchez simply fulfils a doctor's prognosis;[5] and in "Incredible Story" the grandmother's death provides no liberation for Eréndira and

109

Ulises, at least in no obvious way, since Eréndira disappears and abandons Ulises. In both stories, therefore, the death/departure is a satisfactory termination without providing a definitive step forward or insight.

"Drowned Man" and "Last Journey" offer a different, more causal structure. "Drowned Man," it is true, does end with a departure— Esteban is thrown back into the sea, he is given a second burial—but, as well as representing the end of a cultural cycle (the preparation of a body for burial), it also marks a moment of crucial insight for the villagers. The whole story is based on the single task of preparing the body for burial—this gives it a tighter integration than most of the other stories—and therefore the ending, the burial, is a culmination, is a climax directly related to the preceding events and given extra weight by the coincidental resolution of the villagers to change their outlook on life. Similarly, "Last Journey" has a climactic ending (this time with no departure motif) which is the direct outcome of a particular resolution brought to fruition. By contrast, the ending of "Very Old Man" (not untypically) seems to be underdetermined; it is pointless to ask why the bird-man's feathers grow and why he flies away, since there is no cause other than the need to provide a narrative ending.

This type of ending leaves us with a global structure as a basis for most of the stories: arrival–reaction and expansion–departure. But the symmetry of this structure is deceptively attractive. It is deceptive because it provides a neat representation which fails to take into account an important aspect of the stories: their elusiveness. It is not that this structure is wrong, simply that it does not tell us enough. Above all, this pattern seems "closed," where the stories are teasingly "open"— that is, they are thematically reticent while foregrounding elements of a highly imaginative and problematic sort. There is a need, therefore, to question any simple, closed representation. One way to modify the neatness of the first representation is by looking at the reversals which contribute to the instability of the stories; and one way to begin trying to make sense of their openness—without reducing the stories to statements of what they are "about," which would impose closure from "outside"—is to examine the fair motif.

The reversals in *ISS* consist of transpositions of a limited number of initial ideas into new configurations. This is a consistent trend and "Blacamán" will serve as a first example of it. The crucial reversal here concerns power. Blacamán's initial position of authority over the narrator is inverted by the end of the story—where Blacamán was strong and cruel, the narrator becomes so. And this is emphasized by the repetition of certain details: at the end the narrator gives a public performance by the sea at Santa María del Darién (pp. 92–3) just as Blacamán does at the very start (pp. 83–5), and he uses exactly the same forms of words as Blacamán.[6] Clearly there is a comprehensive reversal here, and it is inseparable from repetition; there is a repetition of forms with variation of agents or characters; in other words, substantial repetition of detail is accompanied by strategic variation, and both repetition and variation are crucial to the existence of the reversal. Here we find some of the paradoxical complexity of *ISS*: the narrative line depends on forms of repetition, the repetition involves strategic variation, and strategic variation helps constitute reversal.

"Last Journey" also depends on interlocking repetitions and reversals. And this is not simply a matter of people's believing the narrator at the end where they do not do so for the bulk of the story. Belief/disbelief *is* an important polarity, but there are also others: not seeing/seeing, dark/light, silence/sound, illusion/reality. Now the story is advanced by annual repetitions of the same events: the town and the narrator's mother do not see the shipwreck, but the narrator does; the narrator believes that the silent shipwreck is real, but others believe it is an illusion. These polarities are reinforced by the unexpected effects of darkness and light; though it arrives at night the ship shows no light as it passes the lighted buoys in the bay, and it is visible to the narrator only when the lighthouse throws no light on it (p. 73). But the final repetition introduces multiple variations and repetitions: the positions of light and darkness are inverted—the lights on the ship suddenly blaze as the lights on the buoys go out; the ship produces normal noises (from engines and passengers); and the whole town sees the shipwreck—it happens as a real, shared experience. So the experience is repeated again, but only partially; the shipwreck is broadly the same for the narrator (only light and sound differ), but it is totally different for other people—in other words, it takes place. There is a reversal, and one which abolishes the polarities which seemed to define the initial conflict; there is a repetition with major variations, the elements being thrown into a new configuration, displaced not enough to obscure the repetition of a general framework, but enough to resemanticize it. Again there is a slightly paradoxical structure since the narrative thread relies on repetition, and that repetition contributes to the existence of reversals, and both repetition and reversal seem to run counter to the notion of narrative thread, suggesting a process of return or folding back rather than of forward movement.

The sheer variety of the reversal/repetition structures will be evident by looking at a final example. At the start of "Constant Death" the positions of the two main characters are as follows: Onésimo Sánchez, the senator seeking re-election, is a man with power, an insider from the legal point of view, a man with a certain future, namely imminent death; Nelson Farina is a man with a guilty past because of death (he has murdered his wife) and this makes him an outsider legally speaking, a man with an uncertain future. Preceding the events in the story is a past of interaction between Farina and Sánchez—Farina has repeatedly petitioned Sánchez for a false identity card to put him on the right side of the law, and he has been unsuccessful; by contrast, Sánchez has himself repeatedly petitioned the town's voters for their support in elections and been successful. This pattern of polarities in the past is a crucial point of reference for the events in the story. The events repeat and vary those of the past. This time Sánchez is dogged by recent news of his own impending death, it dominates him as death has formerly dominated Farina, and it alters the course of his day-to-day life: his decision-making is affected and also his attitude to others; this is a reversal of his former position. But there is also repetition here in so far as Farina petitions Sánchez again, tempting him with his daughter, Laura, and this time he is successful since he acquires legal, insider status and a safe future, a reversal of his former position. Sánchez acquires Laura, but their relationship causes scandal—they are social outsiders as Farina was before. So the positions are reversed, though the basic detail and points of reference (death, legality, past/future) are repeated. The narrative has moved forward, but it has done so by going back. In this story and others the attractiveness of reversals for the structure is surely that they obviate the need to introduce external or new factors—the focus of a story is tightly delimited to a working out or exploitation of given material, and that circumscribes and minimizes the scope of a story: a first principle of the genre. Moreover, reversals also provide a strong sense of balance—the process of reconfiguration achieves a clear impression of completeness, of a movement finished, of an absolute realignment not susceptible to further modification. Clearly this reinforces the "sense of an ending" in some stories as an addition to the departure motif discussed on pp. 122–3.

There remains the question of *ISS*'s thematic reticence. How might some thematic focus be located? This is an especially acute question in so far as *Big Mama's Funeral* shows a consistent focus on human confrontation, on the nature of human resourcefulness, and even (implicitly) on psychology; with the exception of "Big Mama's Funeral," that collection shows little of the festive expansiveness of *ISS*, which is nearer the status of "pure fiction." But to talk of "reticence" is not another way of describing "emptiness," that is, a way of saying "these stories are simple *divertissements*." The apparently closed, linear pattern—arrival–reaction and expansion–departure—in its sheer visibility can suggest the need to probe more deeply into the stories; that linear pattern may be visible in inverse proportion to the "visibility" of meaning—in this case, to isolate structures is clearly not to have exhausted the stories. Derrida states this point with clarity in an early essay: "the relief and design of structures appears more clearly when content, which is the living energy of meaning, is neutralized."[7] The word "expansion" which I have used might give further pause for thought, suggesting as it does an openness which formal analysis may overlook. The idea of openness is precisely what the fair motif tends to foreground.

The fair motif is, or accompanies, an intrusion into the narrative space in *ISS*—it constitutes or reinforces a radical disequilibrium in life patterns; in this way it represents a potential opening or transformation. And in that connection the fair motif can be examined in the light of what Bakhtin calls popular-festive forms or carnivals. Bakhtin's theorization is useful:

> Carnival is a pageant without a stage and without a division into performers and spectators. In the carnival everyone is an active participant, everyone communes in the carnival act. Carnival is not contemplated, it is, strictly speaking, not even played out; its participants *live* in it, they live according to its laws, as long as those laws are in force, i.e., they live a *carnivalistic life*. The carnivalistic life is life drawn out of its *usual rut*, it is to a degree "life turned inside out," "life the wrong way round" ("monde à l'envers").
>
> The laws, prohibitions and restrictions which determine the system and order of normal, i.e. non-carnival, life are for the period of carnival suspended; above all, the hierarchical system and all the connected forms of fear, awe, piety, etiquette, etc. are suspended, i.e. everything that is determined by social-hierarchical inequality among people, or any other form of inequality, including age. (pp. 100–1)

Carnival celebrates change itself, the very process of replaceability
. . . (p. 103)[8]

The stress here is on newness, on the potential for change, on living
in a radically different way from before, if only for the duration of the
festivity. In that perspective the fairs or carnivals of *ISS* are recognizable as stimuli for change ("Sea" and "Very Old Man") or as ways of
life ("Blacamán" and "Incredible Story").

But the key question is: "How much really changes or is transformed
in *ISS*?" The answer is that there is some variation. In "Very Old Man"
there is real transformation; the fair builds on and exceeds the arbitrary
arrival of the bird-man and it helps Pelayo and Elisenda to gain new
social status by allowing them to earn money from the curiosity the
bird-man is. Here the change outlasts the festivity. Sánchez in "Constant Death" arrives accompanied by the trappings of a fair and again
life's normality is pushed aside and things are transformed; the special,
carnivalesque circumstances aid the reversal in fortunes of Farina and
Sánchez. But there is also a passage in the story showing another, tem-
porary, transformation, the rare contact between the man of power and
the people. Sánchez ostentatiously moves among them dispensing limited largesse in order to win their support. Here is an important transformation, as the people's power—their vote—is solicited and a
utopian future is promised. Sánchez is briefly in need and the people's
need are satisfied by his bestowing gifts. This passage is entirely in the
spirit of the carnival defined by Bakhtin.

In "Blacamán" the narrator's life is transformed by Blacamán's carnivalesque existence—his talent for resurrection is discovered and that
brings him wealth and apparently satisfaction too. The intrusion of
Esteban in "Drowned Man" stimulates carnivalesque activity which
leads to the long-term transformation of the villagers' attitudes—they
become industrious and productive as never before. By contrast, in
"Incredible Story" the characters are the fair, but no clear transformation is effected; and in "Sea" the fair takes over people's lives but only
temporarily. And this last case is perhaps the most interesting since in
some details it comes closest to Bakhtin's description; for in "Sea" the
fair covers a certain period of time and then disappears leaving things
as before, and this pattern is clearly that of the real carnivals that
Bakhtin describes. In Bakhtin's theory the promise of social reorgani-
zation, of new futures, of hierarchies levelled is not sustained. In *ISS*
there is no clear social implication to the transformations effected, but

these transformations *are* sustained in several cases—the fair/carnival is not simply an institutionalized release of frustration, a circumscribed, annual event; openings are responded to and the carnival impulse is not always lost. And this impulse does alert the reader to a certain thematic focus and consistency throughout, without providing definite propositions or monopolizing attention.

Notes

1. Titles and abbreviations were translated by the writer and differ slightly from published English translations. *ISS* is used to refer to the entire collection. Page numbers refer to the Spanish edition of *La increíble y triste historia de la cándida Eréndira y de su abuela desalmada* (Buenos Aires: Sudamericana, 1976), 5th edition.

2. In the case of "Incredible Story" it might be argued that there is a second arrival of equal significance when Ulises appears in section three; it is not just that he has such striking looks, but also that the relationship that develops between him and Eréndira is crucial to the story's structure.

3. The reference to his "new, deep, man's voice" (p. 73) is an obvious sign of newly gained maturity.

4. The etymology of the word "carnival" seems to suggest that it derives from Latin "carnem levare," to put away flesh or "carne vale," farewell to flesh—the Roman carnival being celebrated just before the fasting of Lent. The word is now loosely interchangeable with the word "fair."

5. The ending may be a piece of ironic play with Francisco de Quevedo's sonnet "Amor constante más allá de la muerte" ("Constant Love beyond Death"): not only does García Márquez invert Quevedo's title, but where the sonnet ends with a declaration that the poet's love can survive even death, the story ends by showing the unavoidably destructive effect a corrupt politician's death has on his love.

6. The interlocking of positions is emphasized by the references to good and bad in the story. At an early stage the narrator establishes a distinction between himself and Blacamán: "That's how he was Blacamán, the bad, because the good one is me" (p. 86). And yet the title of the story refers to Blacamán as "the good," which leads one to transfer "the bad" to the narrator as well, especially as he is as much torturer in the end as Blacamán was at the beginning.

7. Jacques Derrida, "Force and Signification," in *Writing and Difference*, trans. Alan Bass (London, 1981), 5.

8. Mikhail Bakhtin, *Problems of Dostoevsky's Poetics*, trans. R. W. Rotsen (Ann Arbor, 1973).

Chronology

1927   Gabriel José García Márquez born on 6 March in Aracataca.

1928   Violent banana workers' strike in coastal region, later a central theme in his fiction.

1940–1942   Attends Colegio San José in Barranquilla.

1946   Completes secondary education at the Colegio Nacional in the inland city of Zipaquirá.

1947   Enters law school of the National University in Bogotá. Publishes first short story, "La tercera resignación" ("The Third Resignation"), in *El Espectador.*

1948   Assassination of Liberal party leader Jorge Eliécer Gaitán plunges Colombia into chaos. Goes to Cartagena to continue law studies and work as a reporter for *El Universal.* Continues to write and publish short stories.

1950   Moves to Barranquilla to join staff of the newspaper *El Heraldo,* where he writes a column and continues to produce short stories.

1952   "El invierno" (Winter) published in *El Heraldo.* "Monólogo de Isabel viendo llover en Macondo" ("Monologue of Isabel Watching It Rain in Macondo") contains the first mention of the name Macondo.

1954   Returns to Bogotá to do film reviews and editorials for *El Espectador.*

1955   Writes series of 14 articles, later published as *Relato de un náufrago* (*The Story of a Shipwrecked Sailor*). Publishes first novel, *La hojarasca* (*Leaf Storm*). Wins the Concurso Nacional de Cuento short story prize and goes to Europe as a correspondent for *El Espectador.* Newspaper is closed by the Rojas Pinilla dictatorship. Stranded in Paris, he continues to write fiction.

1957   Travels to Eastern Europe, where he writes a series of 10 articles for newspapers.

1958   Arrives in Caracas to work for the newspaper *El Momento*. Marries Mercedes Barcha. Writes most of the stories to appear in *Los funerales de la Mamá Grande* (*Big Mama's Funeral*) in 1962.

1959   Begins work for Cuba's Prensa Latina in Bogotá and later in New York.

1961   Publishes second novel, *El coronel no tiene quien le escriba* (*No One Writes to the Colonel*). Makes bus trip through the Deep South to visit Faulkner country.

1962   Publishes *Big Mama's Funeral* and *La mala hora* (*In Evil Hour*).

1967   *Cien años de soledad* (*One Hundred Years of Solitude*) published in Buenos Aires. Receives the Chianchiano Prize in Italy two years later.

1970   *One Hundred Years of Solitude* appears in English. *Time* magazine calls it one of the 12 best books of the year.

1972   Publishes *La increíble y triste historia de la cándida Eréndira y de su abuela desalmada* (*The Incredible and Sad Tale of Innocent Eréndira and Her Heartless Grandmother*). Receives the Rómulo Gallego Prize and the Neustadt Prize from *Books Abroad*.

1973   Publishes *Cuando era feliz e indocumentado* (*When I Was Happy and Undocumented*), a collection of writings in journalism from the late 1950s.

1975   Publishes *El otoño del patriarca* (*The Autumn of the Patriarch*).

1981   Publishes *Crónica de una muerte anunciada* (*Chronicle of a Death Foretold*) in simultaneous editions in Barcelona, Buenos Aires, Mexico City, and Bogotá.

1982   Receives the Nobel Prize in literature. Publishes *El olor de la guayaba* (*The Fragrance of Guava*), a series of conversations with Plinio Apuleyo Mendoza.

1985   Publishes *El amor en los tiempos del cólera* (*Love in the Time of Cholera*) in simultaneous editions on three continents.

1988   English edition of *Love in the Time of Cholera* becomes Book-of-the-Month Club selection. Remains on the *New York Times* best-seller list for many weeks.

1989   Publishes *El general en su laberinto* (*The General in His Labyrinth*), also in simultaneous editions. Releases a series of six films based on his short stories and novels, under the general title *Amores Difíciles* (Dangerous loves). Directs a workshop for 10 Hispanic screenwriters at the Sundance Institute in Utah.

1990   *The General in His Labyrinth* becomes a *New York Times* best-seller.

Selected Bibliography

Primary Works in Spanish

Short Story Collections

Cuatro cuentos. Mexico City: Comunidad Latinoaméricana de Escritores, 1974. Contains "Monólogo de Isabel viendo llover en Macondo," "En este pueblo no hay ladrones," "Los funerales de la Mamá Grande," and "Un hombre muy viejo con unas alas enormes."

Los funerales de la Mamá Grande. Xalapa, Mexico: Editorial Universidad Veracruzana, 1962. Contains "La siesta del martes," "Un día de estos," "En este pueblo no hay ladrones," "La prodigiosa tarde de Baltazar," "La viuda de Montiel," "Un día después del sábado," "Rosas artificiales," and "Los funerales de la Mamá Grande."

La increíble y triste historia de la cándida Eréndira y de su abuela desalmada. Barcelona: Barral Editores, 1972. Contains "Un señor muy viejo con unas alas enormes," "El mar del tiempo perdido," "El ahogado más hermoso del mundo," "Muerte constante más allá del amor," "El último viaje del buque fantasma," "Blacamán el bueno vendedor de milagros," and "La increíble y triste historia de la cándida Eréndira y de su abuela desalmada."

Isabel viendo llover en Macondo. Buenos Aires: Estuario, 1967. This edition also contains "Los cuentos de Gabriel García Márquez o el trópico desembrujado," by Ernesto Volkening.

El negro que hizo esperar a los ángeles. Montevideo: Ediciones Alfil, 1972. Publication not authorized by García Márquez. Contains "Nabo, el negro que hizo esperar a los ángeles," "Alguien desordena estas rosas," "La mujer que llegaba a las seis," "Ojos de perro azul," Diálogo del espejo," "Amargura para tres sonámbulos," "Eva está dentro de su gato," "La otra costilla de la muerte," and "La tercera resignación."

Ojos de perro azul: nueve cuentos desconocidos. Rosario, Argentina: Equiseditorial, 1972. Contains "La tercera resignación," "La otra costilla de la muerte," "Eva está dentro de su gato," "Amargura para tres sonámbulos," "Diálogo del espejo," "Ojos de perro azul," "La mujer que llegaba a las seis," "Nabo, el negro que hizo esperar a los ángeles," "Alguien desordena estas rosas," "La noche de los alcaravanes," and "Monólogo de Isabel viendo llover en Macondo."

El rastro de tu sangre en la nieve; El verano feliz de la señora Forbes. Bogotá: William Dampier, 1982. This collection has also appeared as *El verano feliz de la Señora Forbes.* Madrid: Almarabu, 1982.

Relato de un naufrago . . . Barcelona: Tusquets, 1970. Based on a series of 14 newspaper accounts published in *El Espectador* in 1955.

Todos los cuentos de Gabriel García Márquez (1947–1972). Barcelona: Plaza & Janés, 1975. Contains the stories from *Ojos de perro azul, Los funerales de la Mamá Grande,* and *La increíble y triste historia de la cándida Eréndira y de su abuela desalmada.*

Uncollected Stories

"Cuentecillo policiaco." *El Heraldo,* 10 June 1950, 3. Written under the pseudonym Septimus.

"El cuento de los generales que se creyeron su propio cuento." *El País* [Madrid], 9 December 1980.

"De como Natanael hace una visita." *Crónica* 2 (6 May 1950): 5, 12.

"Elegía." *El Heraldo,* 1 September 1952, 3. Written under the pseudonym Septimus.

"Final de Natanael." *El Heraldo,* 13 October 1950, 3. Written under the pseudonym Septimus.

"Un hombre viene bajo la lluvia." *El Espectador,* Suplemento Dominical 317, 9 May 1954, 16, 31.

"El muerto alegre." *El Espectador* 312 (4 April 1954).

"La pesadilla." *El Heraldo,* 16 June 1950, 3.

"Pesadillas." *El Heraldo,* 13 July 1950, 3. Written under the pseudonym Septimus.

"Un profesional de la pesadilla." *El Heraldo,* 11 October 1950, 3. Written under the pseudonym Septimus.

"Los signos oscuros." *Revista de la Universidad de México* 16 (September 1961): 6–7.

"Tubal-Caín forja una estrella." *El Espectador,* Fin de Semana 97 (17 January 1948): 8.

Uncollected Short Fiction in Series

APUNTES PARA UNA NOVELA

"La casa de los Buendía." *Crónica* 6 (3 June 1950): 8–9.
"La hija del coronel." *El Heraldo,* 13 June 1950, 3.
"El hijo del coronel." *El Heraldo,* 23 June 1950, 3.
"El regreso de Meme." *El Heraldo,* 22 November 1950, 3.
"Apuntes." *El Heraldo,* 9 January 1951, 3.
"Otros apuntes." *El Heraldo,* 10 January 1951, 3.

LA MARQUESA SERIES

"El elefante de la marquesa." *El Heraldo*, 12 April 1950, 3.
"La marquesa y la silla maravillosa." *El Heraldo*, 19 April 1950, 3.
"Las rectificaciones de la marquesa." *El Heraldo*, 26 April 1950, 3.
"Carta abierta a la marquesa." *El Heraldo*, 3 May 1950, 3.
"Primera respuesta de la marquesa." *El Heraldo*, 10 May 1950, 3.
"Será de Boris realmente?" *El Heraldo*, 11 May 1950, 3.
"Inexplicable ubicuidad de Boris." *El Heraldo*, 17 May 1950, 3.
"El hindú y el desconcierto de la marquesa." *El Heraldo*, 31 May 1950, 3.
"Ja!" *El Heraldo*, 26 May 1950, 3.
"El final necesario." *El Heraldo*, 7 June 1950, 3.

LA SIERPE SERIES

"La Sierpe I. Un país en la Costa Atlántica—I." *Lámpara* 1, no. 5 (November–
    December 1952): 15–18. Seven vignettes republished in *El Espectador*
    during March 1954.
"La herencia sobrenatural de la Marquesita." *El Espectador*, Suplemento Do-
    minical 310, 21 March 1954, 17, 27.
"La extraña idolatría de la Sierpe." *El Espectador*, Suplemento Dominical 311,
    28 March 1954, 17, 30.

Novels and Other Works

El amor en los tiempos del cólera. Bogotá: La Oveja Negra, 1985; Mexico City:
    Diana, 1985; Buenos Aires: Sudamericana, 1985; Barcelona: Bruguera,
    1985.
El asalto. Managua: Nueva Nicaragua, 1983. Originally published as *Viva San-
    dino* and subsequently as *El secuestro*.
Así es Caracas. Caracas: Ateneo de Caracas, 1980.
La aventura de Miguel Littín, clandestino en Chile. Bogotá: La Oveja Negra, 1986.
Chile, el golpe y los gringos. Bogotá: Editorial Latina, 1974.
Cien años de soledad. Buenos Aires: Sudamericana, 1967.
El coronel no tiene quien le escriba. Medellín: Aguirre, 1958.
Crónica de una muerte anunciada. Bogotá: La Oveja Negra, 1981; Mexico City:
    Diana, 1981; Buenos Aires: Sudamericana, 1981; Barcelona: Bruguera,
    1981.
Crónicas y reportajes. Bogotá: Instituto Colombiano de Cultura, 1976. Articles
    published in *El Espectador*.
Cuando era feliz e indocumentado. Caracas: El Ojo del Camello, 1973. Articles
    published in the Caracas press.

Cuba en Angola. Tegucigalpa: R. Amaya Amador, 1977.

De viaje por los países socialistas: 90 días en la "Cortina de Hierro." 5th ed. Bogotá: La Oveja Negra, 1980.

El general en su laberinto. Bogotá: La Oveja Negra, 1989; Buenos Aires: Sudamericana, 1989; Madrid: Mondadori, 1989; Mexico City: Diana, 1989.

La hojarasca. Bogotá: Sipa, 1955.

La mala hora. Madrid: Taller de Gráficas Luis Péerz, 1962. Edition rejected by García Márquez. Mexico City: Era, 1966. Edition accepted by García Márquez as the first.

Obra periodística. Edited by Jacques Gilard. Barcelona: Bruguera, 1981–84. Vol. 1, *Textos costeños;* Vols. 2–3, *Entre cachacos;* Vol. 4, *De Europa y América.*

Operación Carlota. Lima: Mosca Azul, 1977.

El otoño del patriarca. Barcelona: Plaza & Janés, 1975; Buenos Aires: Sudamericana, 1975.

Periodismo militante. Bogotá: Son de Máquina, 1978.

Persecución y muerte de minorías. Dos perspectivas polemicas. Buenos Aires: Juárez, 1984. With Guillermo Nolano-Juárez.

Los Sandinistas. Bogota: La Oveja Negra, 1979. Documents and reports by Gabriel García Márquez and others.

El secuestro: relato cinematográfico. Salamanca: Lóguez, 1983. Film script.

English Translations of Primary Works

Short Fiction

Collected Stories. Translated by Gregory Rabassa and S. J. Bernstein. New York: Harper & Row, 1984. Contains these short stories from *Ojos de perro azul:* "The Third Resignation," "The Other Side of Death," "Eva Is Inside Her Cat," "Bitterness for Three Sleepwalkers," "Dialogue with the Mirror," "Eyes of a Blue Dog," "The Woman Who Came at Six O'Clock," "Nabo: The Black Man Who Made the Angels Wait," "Someone Has Been Disarranging These Roses," "The Night of the Curlews," and "Monologue of Isabel Watching It Rain in Macondo." Short stories from *Los funerales de la Mamá Grande* are "Tuesday Siesta," "One of These Days," "There Are No Thieves in This Town," "Balthazar's Marvelous Afternoon," "Montiel's Widow," "One Day after Saturday," "Artificial Roses," and "Big Mama's Funeral." From *La incréible y triste historia de la cándida Eréndira . . .* the following short stories are included: "A Very Old Man with Enormous Wings," "The Sea of Lost Time," "The Handsomest Drowned Man in the World," "Death Constant beyond Love," "The Last Voyage of the Ghost Ship," "Blacamán the Good, Vendor of Miracles," "The Incredible and Sad Tale of Innocent Eréndira and Her Heartless Grandmother."

Innocent Eréndira and Other Stories. Translated by Gregory Rabassa. New York: Harper & Row, 1978. Contains "The Incredible and Sad Tale of Innocent Eréndira and Her Heartless Grandmother," "The Sea of Lost Time," "Death Constant beyond Love," "The Third Resignation," "The Other Side of Death," "Eva Is Inside Her Cat," "Dialogue with the Mirror," "Bitterness for Three Sleepwalkers," "Eyes of a Blue Dog," "The Woman Who Came at Six O'Clock," "Someone Has Been Disarranging These Roses," and "The Night of the Curlews."

"Leaf Storm" and Other Stories. Translated by Gregory Rabassa. New York: Harper & Row, 1972. Contains, in addition to the novel, "The Handsomest Drowned Man in the World," "A Very Old Man with Enormous Wings," "Blacamán the Good, Vendor of Miracles," "The Last Voyage of the Ghost Ship," "Monologue of Isabel Watching It Rain in Macondo," and "Nabo."

No One Writes to the Colonel and Other Stories. Translated by J. S. Bernstein. New York: Harper & Row, 1968. Contains, in addition to the novel, "Tuesday Siesta," "One of These Days," "There Are No Thieves in This Town," "Balthazar's Marvelous Afternoon," "Montiel's Widow," "One Day after Saturday," "Artificial Roses," and "Big Mama's Funeral."

The Story of a Shipwrecked Sailor. Translated by Randolph Hogan. New York: Knopf, 1986.

Novels and Other Works

The Autumn of the Patriarch. Translated by Gregory Rabassa. New York: Harper & Row, 1976.

Chronicle of a Death Foretold. Translated by Gregory Rabassa. New York: Knopf, 1982.

The Fragrance of Guava. London: Verso, 1983. With Plinio Apuleyo Mendoza.

The General in His Labyrinth. Translated by Edith Grossman. New York: Knopf, 1990.

In Evil Hour. Translated by Gregory Rabassa. New York: Harper & Row, 1979.

Love in the Time of Cholera. Translated by Edith Grossman. New York: Knopf, 1988.

One Hundred Years of Solitude. Translated by Gregory Rabassa. New York: Harper & Row, 1970.

Secondary Works

Interviews

Dreifus, Claudia. "*Playboy* Interview: Gabriel García Márquez." *Playboy,* 2 February 1983, 65–77, 172–78.

Durán, Armando. "Conversations with Gabriel García Márquez." *Review 70* 3 (1971): 109–18.

Guibert, Rita. *Seven Voices: Seven Latin American Writers Talk to Rita Guibert.* New York: Knopf, 1973. 303–37.

Kennedy, William. "The Yellow Trolley Car in Barcelona and Other Visions: A Profile of Gabriel García Márquez." *Atlantic,* January 1973, 50–58.

Lorenz, Gunter. *Dialog mit Lateinamerika.* Tubingen: Horst Edmann Verlag, 1970.

La novela en América Latina: Diálogo. Lima: Carlos Milla Batres, 1968. With Mario Vargas Llosa.

El olor de la guayaba. Conversación con Plinio Apuleyo Mendoza. Barcelona: Bruguera, 1982; Bogotá: La Oveja Negra, 1982; Mexico City: Diana, 1982. Translated by Ann Wright as *The Fragrance of Guava.* London: Verso Editions, 1983.

Rentería Mantilla, Alfonso, ed. *García Márquez habla de García Márquez, 33 reportajes.* Bogotá: Rentería Mantilla, 1979.

Rodman, Selden. *Tongues of Fallen Angels,* 113–33. New York: New Directions, 1972.

Simons, Marlise. "Love and Age: A Talk with García Márquez." *New York Times Book Review,* 7 April 1985, 1, 18–19.

———. "A Talk with Gabriel García Márquez." *New York Times Book Review,* 5 December 1982, 7, 60–61.

Stone, Peter S. "Gabriel García Márquez." In *Writers at Work: The "Paris Review" Interviews,* edited by George Plimpton, 313–39. New York: Viking Press, 1984.

Books

Bell-Villada, Gene H. *García Márquez: The Man and His Work.* Chapel Hill: University of North Carolina Press, 1990.

Carrillo, Germán Darío. *La narrativa de Gabriel García Márquez.* Madrid: Ediciones de Arte y Bibliografía, 1975.

Earle, Peter, ed. *Gabriel García Márquez.* Madrid: Taurus, 1981.

Fau, Margaret Eustella. *Gabriel García Márquez: An Annotated Bibliography, 1947–1979.* Westport, Conn.: Greenwood Press, 1980.

Fau, Margaret Eustella, and Nelly Sfeir de González. *Bibliographic Guide to Gabriel García Márquez, 1979–1985.* Westport, Conn.: Greenwood Press, 1986.

Giacoman, Helmy, ed. *Homenaje a Gabriel García Márquez: Variaciones interpretivas en torno a su obra.* New York: Las Américas, 1972.

Harss, Luis, and Barbara Dohmann. *Into the Mainstream.* New York: Harper & Row, 1967.

Hernández de López, Ana María, ed. *En el punto de mira: Gabriel García Márquez.* Madrid: Pliegos, 1985.

———. *Interpretaciones a la obra de García Márquez.* Monografías de ALDEEU. Madrid: Beramar, 1986.

Janes, Regina. *Gabriel García Márquez: Revolutions in Wonderland.* Columbia: University of Missouri Press, 1981.

McGuirk, Bernard, and Richard Cardwell, eds. *Gabriel García Márquez: New Readings.* Cambridge: Cambridge University Press, 1987.

McMurray, George R., ed. *Critical Essays on Gabriel García Márquez.* Boston: G. K. Hall, 1987.

———. *Gabriel García Márquez.* New York: Frederick Ungar, 1977.

———. *Gabriel García Márquez: Life, Work, and Criticism.* Fredericton, New Brunswick: York Press, 1987.

McNerney, Kathleen. *Understanding Gabriel García Márquez.* Columbia: University of South Carolina Press, 1989.

Martínez, Pedro Simón, ed. *Sobre García Márquez.* Montevideo: Biblioteca de Marcha, 1971.

Minta, Stephen. *García Márquez: Writer of Colombia.* New York: Harper & Row, 1987.

Mose, Kenrick. *Defamiliarization in the Work of Gabriel García Márquez.* Lewiston, N.Y.: Edwin Mellen Press, 1989.

Oberhelman, Harley D. *The Presence of Faulkner in the Writings of García Márquez.* Lubbock: Texas Tech Press, 1980.

Sorela, Pedro. *El otro García Márquez: Los años difíciles.* Madrid: Mondadori, 1988.

Vargas Llosa, Mario. *García Márquez: Historia de un deicidio.* Barcelona: Barral Editores, 1971.

Williams, Raymond L. *Gabriel García Márquez.* Boston: Twayne Publishers, 1984.

Zuluaga, Conrado. *Puerta abierta a García Márquez y otras puertas.* Bogotá: La Editora, 1982.

Articles and Chapters in Books

Amoretti H., María. "'Un día de éstos' de García Márquez: Un desafortunado proceso de venganza." *Káñina* 7, no. 1 (January–July 1983): 35–42.

Aponte, Barbara B. "El rito de la iniciación en el cuento hispanoamericano." *Hispanic Review* 51, no. 2 (Spring 1983): 129–46. About "Eréndira."

Arango, Manuel Antonio. "Tema y estructura en el cuento 'La siesta del martes.'" *Thesaurus* 40, no. 3 (September–December 1985): 591–604.

Aronne-Amestoy, Lida. "Blacabunderías del método: El recurso al discurso en García Márquez." In *En el punto de mira: Gabriel García Márquez*, edited by Ana María Hernández de López, 55–62. Madrid: Pliegos, 1985. About "Blacamán el bueno vendedor de milagros."

———. "Fantasía y compromiso en un cuento de Gabriel García Márquez." *Symposium* 38, no. 4 (Winter 1984–85): 287–97. About "El ahogado más hermoso del mundo."

———. *Utopía, paraíso e historia: Inscripciones del mito en García Márquez, Rulfo y Cortázar.* Amsterdam: Benjamins, 1986. About "El ahogado más hermoso del mundo."

Arrigoitia, Luis de. "Tres cuentos de Gabriel García Márquez: 'Monólogo de Isabel viendo llover en Macondo' (1955), 'La siesta del martes' (1957), 'Los funerales de la Mamá Grande' (1959)." *Revista de Estudios Hispánicos* [Puerto Rico] 6 (1979): 131–52.

Arrington, Melvin S., Jr. "'La viuda de Montiel:' Un retrato en miniatura de Macondo." In *En el punto de mira: Gabriel García Márquez*, edited by Ana María Hernández de López, 67–69. Madrid: Pliegos, 1985.

Benítez Rojo, Antonio, and Hilda O. Benítez. "Eréndira liberada: La subversión del mito del macho occidental." *Revista Iberoamericana* 128–29 (July–December 1984): 1057–75.

———. "Eréndira, o la Bella Durmiente de García Márquez." *Cuadernos Hispanoamericanos* 448 (October 1987): 31–48.

Benson, John. "Literatura y periodismo de García Márquez: La Mamá Grande y la gran mamá." *Explicación de Textos Literarios* 15, no. 1 (1986–87): 21–31.

Berroa, Rei. "Sobre 'Muerte constante más allá del amor.'" *Discurso Literario* 1, no. 1 (Fall 1983): 5–15.

Boo, Matilde L. "'La increíble y triste historia de la cándida Eréndira y de su abuela desalmada,' de García Márquez, y *Tormento* de Galdós: Significación irónico de la irrealidad." In *En el punto de mira: Gabriel García Márquez*, edited by Ana María Hernández de López, 71–82. Madrid: Pliegos, 1985.

Borgeson, Paul W., Jr. "Los pobres ángeles de Gabriel García Márquez y Joaquín Pasos." *Crítica Hispánica* 3, no. 2 (1981): 111–23. About "Un hombre muy viejo con unas alas enormes."

Burgos, Fernando. "El cuento como épica de la imaginación en García Márquez." In *En el punto de mira: Gabriel García Márquez*, edited by Ana María Hernández de López, 91–102. Madrid: Pliegos, 1985. About "Eréndira."

———. "Hacia el centro de la imaginación: *La increíble y triste historia de la cándida Eréndira y de su abuela desalmada.*" *INTI: Revista de Literatura Hispánica* 16–17 (1982–83): 70–81.

Selected Bibliography

Byk, John. "From Fact to Fiction: Gabriel García Márquez and the Short Story." *Mid-American Review* 6, no. 2 (1986): 111–16.

Castillo, Debra A. "The Storyteller and the Carnival Queen: 'Funerales de la Mamá Grande.'" *Romance Quarterly* 35, no. 4 (November 1988): 457–67.

Chase, Cida S. "'La Violencia' and Political Violence in García Márquez's Short Fiction." *Journal of Popular Culture* 22, no. 1 (Summer 1988): 73–82.

Chase, Victoria F. "De mitificación en 'Los funerales de la Mamá Grande.'" *Texto Crítico* [Xalapa, Mexico] 6, no. 16–17 (January–June 1980): 233–47.

Cjamdadu, Amaryll B. "Las soledades y los solitarios en *La increíble y triste historia de la cándida Eréndira y de su abuela desalmada* de Gabriel García Márquez." *Symposium* 40, no. 4 (Winter 1986–87): 297–307.

Clark, John R. "Angel in Excrement: García Márquez's Innocent Tale ('A Very Old Man with Enormous Wings')." *Notes on Contemporary Literature* 18, no. 3 (May 1988): 2–3.

Coover, Robert. "The Master's Voice." *American Review* 26 (November 1977): 361–88.

Dauster, Frank. "The Short Stories of García Márquez." *Books Abroad* 43, no. 3 (Summer 1973): 466–70.

Davis, Mary E. "The Voyage beyond the Map: 'El ahogado más hermoso del mundo.'" In *Critical Essays on Gabriel García Márquez*, edited by George R. McMurray, 159–68. Boston: G. K. Hall, 1987.

Foster, David William. "The Double Inscription of the *Narrataire* in 'Los funerales de la Mamá Grande.'" In *Studies in the Contemporary Spanish-American Short Story*, 51–62. Columbia: University of Missouri Press, 1979.

———. "García Márquez and the *Ecriture* of Complicity: 'La prodigiosa tarde de Baltazar.'" In *Studies in the Spanish-American Short Story*, 39–50. Columbia: University of Missouri Press, 1979.

Gerlach, John. "The Logic of Wings: García Márquez, Todorov, and the Endless Resources of Fantasy." In *Bridges to Fantasy*. Carbondale: Southern Illinois University Press, 1982.

Gilard, Jacques. "Cronología de los primeros textos literarios de García Márquez (1947–1955)." *Revista de Crítica Literaria Latinoamericana* 2, no. 3 (1976): 95–106.

Goetzinger, Judith. "The Emergence of a Folk Myth in 'Los funerales de la Mamá Grande.'" *Revista de Estudios Hispánicos* [Puerto Rico] 6, no. 2 (May 1972): 237–48.

González, Eduardo. "Beware of Gift-bearing Tales: Reading García Márquez according to Mauss." *Modern Language Notes* 97, no. 2 (March 1982): 347–64.

Grossman, Edith. "The Truth Is Stranger Than Fact." *Review* 30 (September–December 1981): 71–73.

Hancock, Joel. "Gabriel García Márquez's 'Eréndira' and the Brothers Grimm." In *Critical Essays on Gabriel García Márquez*, edited by George R. McMurray, 152–59. Boston: G. K. Hall, 1987.

Hensey, Fritz G. "Differential Stylistics and Alternate Versions of a García Márquez Story." In *Language and Language Use: Studies in Spanish*, ed. Terrell A. Morgan, James F. Lee, and Bill Van Patten, 313–37. Lanham, Md.: University Presses of America, 1987. About "El ahogado más hermoso del mundo."

Jain, Jasbir. "Gabriel García Márquez (Colombia; 1928–)." In *Latin American Writers*, edited by Alok Bhalla, 83–100. New York: Envoy Press, 1987.

Kason, Nancy M. "El arte del ambiente psicológico en 'Un día de éstos.'" In *En el punto de mira: Gabriel García Márquez*, edited by Ana María Hernández de López, 83–90. Madrid: Pliegos, 1985.

Linker, Susan Mott. "Myth and Legend in Two Prodigious Tales of García Márquez." *Hispanic Journal* 9, no. 1 (Fall 1987): 89–100. About "La prodigiosa tarde de Baltazar" and "La viuda de Montiel."

McGrady, Donald. "Acerca de una colección desconocida de relatos por Gabriel García Márquez." *Thesaurus* 27, no. 2 (May–August 1972): 293–320.

Méndez, José Luis. "La dialéctica del amo y el esclavo en 'La cándida Eréndira' de Gabriel García Márquez." *La Torre* 1, no. 1 (January–March 1987): 59–68.

Mendizábal, J. C. "Ceguera clarividente en 'Rosas artificales' de Gabriel García Márquez." *Káñina* 4, no. 1 (January–June 1988): 78–80.

Mendoza, Plinio. "El caso perdido." In *La llama y el hielo*, 9–150. Barcelona: Planeta, 1984.

Miller, Beth. "Alegoría e ideología en 'La prodigiosa tarde de Baltazar': El artista del Tercer Mundo y su producto." *Revista de Crítica Literaria Latinoamericana* 11, no. 23 (1986): 53–62.

Millington, Mark. "Actant and Character in García Márquez's *La increíble y triste historia de la cándida Eréndira y de su abuela desalmada*." In *Essays in Honour of Robert Brian Tate from His Colleagues and Pupils*, edited by R. A. Cardwell, 83–90. Nottingham: University of Nottingham Monographs in the Humanities II, 1984.

———. "Aspects of Narrative Structure in *The Incredible and Sad Story of the Innocent Eréndira and her Heartless Grandmother*." In *Gabriel García Márquez: New Readings*, edited by Bernard McGuirk and Richard Cardwell, 117–33. Cambridge: Cambridge University Press, 1987.

Mora, Gabriela. "'La prodigiosa tarde de Baltazar:' Problemas del significado." *INTI: Revista de Literatura Hispánica* 16–17 (1982–83): 83–92.

Morello Frosch, Marta. "The Common Wonders of García Márquez's Recent Fiction." *Books Abroad* 47, no. 3 (Summer 1973): 496–505.

———. "Función de lo fantástico en 'La increíble y triste historia de la cándida

Eréndira y de su abuela desalmada' de Gabriel García Márquez." *Symposium* 38, no. 4 (Winter 1984–85): 321–30.

Muller-Bergh, Klaus. "*Relato de un naufrago:* Gabriel García Márquez's Tale of Shipwreck and Survival at Sea." *Books Abroad* 47, no. 3 (Summer 1973): 460–66.

Neghme Echeverría, Lidia. "La ironía trágica en un relato de García Márquez." *Eco* [Bogotá] 16 (October 1974): 627–46. About "Muerte constante más allá del amor."

Oberhelman, Harley D. "Gabriel Eligio García habla de Gabito." *Hispania* 61, no. 3 (September 1978): 541–42.

Ortiz, Efren. "'La cándida Eréndira:' Una lectura mítica." *Texto Crítico* [Xalapa, Mexico] 6, no. 16–17 (January–June 1980): 248–54.

Paiewonsky-Conde, Edgar. "La escritura como acto revolucionario: 'Los funerales de la Mamá Grande.'" In *En el punto de mira: Gabriel García Márquez*, edited by Ana María Hernández de López, 33–53. Madrid: Pliegos, 1985.

———. "La parodia como pre-dicción histórica: 'Los funerales de la Mamá Grande.'" *Ideologies and Literature* 2, no. 2 (Fall 1987): 125–43.

Palencia-Roth, Michael. "Entre dos mundos: La cuentística de García Márquez (1968–1972)." *Acta litteraria Academiae Scientiarum Hungaricae* 27, no. 1–2 (1985): 75–98.

Pearson, Lon. "A Previously Ignored Model for García Márquez's Mamá Grande Discovered in His Early Newspaper Writing." *Publications of the Missouri Philological Association* 10 (1985): 35–43.

Peel, Roger M. "The Short Stories of Gabriel García Márquez." *Studies in Short Fiction* 8, no. 1 (Winter 1971): 159–68.

Penuel, Arnold M. "The Theme of Colonialism in García Márquez' 'La increíble y triste historia de la cándida Eréndira y de su abuela desalmada.'" *Hispanic Journal* 10, no. 1 (Fall 1988): 67–83.

Perus, Françoise. "Algunas consideraciones histórico-teóricas para el estudio del cuento." *Plural* 9, no. 189 (16 June 1987): 37–39. About "Los funerales de la Mamá Grande."

Pierce, Robert N. "Fact or Fiction? The Developmental Journalism of Gabriel García Márquez." *Journal of Popular Culture* 22, no. 1 (Summer 1988): 63–71.

Pineda Botero, Alvaro. "Agresión y poesía: A propósito de dos cuentos de García Márquez." *University of Dayton Review* 18, no. 1 (Summer 1986): 59–65. About "La siesta del martes" and "El último viaje del buque fantasma."

Reis, Roberto. "O fantástico do Poder e o Poder do Fantástico." *Ideologies and Literature* 3, no. 13 (June–August 1980): 3–22. About "Eréndira."

Rohter, Larry. "García Márquez: Words into Film." *New York Times*, 13 August 1989 (Arts & Leisure), 1H, 28H.

Sacerio-Garí, Enrique. "Las flores de Borges en García Márquez." *Hispania* 70, no. 1 (March 1987): 62–66. About "Rosas artificiales."

Sims, Robert. "The Creation of Myth in García Márquez' 'Los funerales de la Mamá Grande.'" *Hispania* 61, no. 1 (March 1978): 14–23.

———. "Narrating Violence and the Permutable Violence of Narration: The Evolution of Focalization in the Work of Gabriel García Márquez from 1947 to 1981." *Hispanic Journal* 10, no. 1 (Fall 1988): 53–65.

———. "La serie de La Sierpe de García Márquez: La política de la narración o como narrar la política." *Chasqui* 16, no. 1 (February 1987): 45–53.

———. "Theme, Narrative Bricolage and Myth in García Márquez." *Journal of Spanish Studies: Twentieth Century* 8, no. 1–2 (Spring–Fall 1980): 145–59.

Speratti-Pinero, Emma Susana. "De las fuentes y su utilización en 'El ahogado más hermoso del mundo.'" In *Homenaje a Ana María Barrenechea*, edited by Lia Schwartz Lerner and Isaís Lerner, 549–55. Madrid: Castalia, 1984.

Vargas Llosa, Mario. "A Morbid Prehistory (The Early Stories)." *Books Abroad* 47, no. 3 (Summer 1973): 451–60.

Williams, Raymond L. "An Introduction to the Early Journalism of García Márquez: 1948–1958." *Latin American Literary Review* 13, no. 25 (January–June 1985): 117–32.

———. "Los comienzos de un Premio Nobel: 'La tercera resignación.'" *El Café Literario* 5, no. 29–30 (September–December 1982): 39–41.

Yviricu, Jorge. "Transposición y subversión en 'Un señor muy viejo con unas alas enormes.'" In *From Dante to García Márquez*, edited by Gene H. Bell-Villada, 384–90. Williamstown, Mass.: Williams College, 1987.

Index

"Apuntes para una novela" (Notes for a novel), 16
Amadís de Gaula, 50, 67
Amores difíciles (Dangerous loves—film series), 55
Aracataca, 3, 4, 13, 20, 73, 74, 77
Ariadne (Arídnere), 50
Arrington, Melvin S. Jr., 28
arrival structure, 104–6, 115n2
"Artificial Roses" ("Rosas artificiales"), *30–31*, 102
Association of Colombian Artists and Writers, 28
Asturias, Miguel Angel, 50
Autumn of the Patriarch (*El otoño del patriarca*), 3, 6, 32, 35, 42, 43, 44, 47, 51, 52, 54, 66, 68, 94–96, 97

Bakhtin, Mikhail, 113–15
"Balthazar's Marvelous Afternoon" ("La prodigiosa tarde de Baltazar"), *24–27*, 90, 101
"banana" English, 46
banana massacre, 94
Barranquilla, 4, 5, 10, 64, 66, 76, 84
Barranquilla Group (Grupo de Barranquilla), 10, 16
Bartok, Béla, 68
Berroa, Rei, 43
"Big Mama's Funeral," 6, 28, *31–35*, 103, 113
"Bitterness for Three Sleepwalkers" ("Amargura para tres sonámbulos"), 8, 12, 90, 93, 96
"Blacamán the Good, Vendor of Miracles" ("Blacamán el bueno vendedor de milagros"), *46–48*, 50, 104, 105, 106, 108, 110–11, 114, 115n6

Blasco Ibáñez, Vicente: "El hallazgo" ("The Windfall"), 100
Bogotá, 4, 7
Bolívar, Simón, 55
Borges, Jorge Luis, 31
Burgos, Fernando, 51
Burroughs, Edgar Rice: *Tarzan of the Apes*, 67

Caldwell, Erskine, 78
Camus, Albert, 79
carnivalization technique, 37, 38, 41, 45, 47, 51, 83, *113–15*
Carrillo, Germán D., 48
Cartagena (de Indias), 5, 7, 10, 44, 84
Cepeda Samudio, Alvaro, 48
Chronicle of a Death Foretold (*Crónica de una muerte anunciada*), 54
Columbus, Christopher: *The Diary of Christopher Columbus*, 70
"committed" literature, 71
Conrad, Joseph, 67
Conservative party, 4
Cortés, Fernando, 57n3
Cuando era feliz e indocumentado (When I was happy and undocumented), 88
curlews, 58n12, 94

Dauster, Frank, 13
Davis, Mary E., 41, 42
"Death Constant beyond Love" ("Muerte constante más allá del amor"), *42–44*, 46, 50, 104, 106, 107, 109, 112, 114
Defoe, Daniel: *A Journal of the Plague Year*, 67
Derrida, Jacques, 113

"Dialogue with the Mirror" ("Diálogo del espejo"), 7, 93, 99
Dreifus, Claudia, 63

El Espectador, (newspaper), 5, 6, 7, 10, 16–17, 53, 54, 88
El Heraldo (newspaper), 10, 13
El Momento (newspaper), 19
encomienda (land tenure system), 32, 59n29
Escalona, Rafael, 48
Espronceda, José de, 68
"Eva Is Inside Her Cat" ("Eva está dentro de su gato"), 5, 6, 15, 90, 92, 99
"Eyes of a Blue Dog" ("Ojos de perro azul"), 8–9, 90, 93

Faulkner, William, 4, 10, 19, 42, 53, 55, 57n9, 77, 85, 97, 98; *The Sound and the Fury,* 11–12
Foster, David William, 32, 34
Foundation for the New Latin American Film, 55
Fuenmayor, Alfonso, 9
Fuenmayor, José Félix, 10

Gaitán, Jorge Eliécer, 4, 19, 20; *see also "la violencia"*
García, Gabriel Eligio (father), 57n3
García Márquez, Gabriel: childhood of, 4, 20, 73; early short stories, 5–15, 83; education of, 4; journalism and, 15–16, 65, 72, 79, 83, 84–89; solitude in, 76, 91, 92

WORKS—NOVELS AND
COLLECTIONS
Autumn of the Patriarch, The (El otoño del patriarca), 3, 6, 32, 35, 42, 43, 44, 47, 51, 52, 54, 66, 68, 94–96, 97
Chronicle of a Death Foretold (Crónica de una muerte anunciada), 54
Cuando era feliz e indocumentado (When I was happy and undocumented), 88

Fragrance of Guava, The (El olor de la guavaba), 63
General in His Labyrinth, The (El general en su laberinto), 55
In Evil Hour (La mala hora), 19, 22, 24, 28, 30, 94, 98, 100–101
"Leaf Storm" and Other Stories (La hojarasca), 6, 10, 12, 13, 16, 19, 20, 28, 29, 64, 74, 90, 91, 94, 96, 97, 98
Love in the Time of Cholera (El amor en los tiempos del cólera), 3, 44, 54, 55
"No One Writes to the Colonel" and Other Stories (El coronel no tiene quien le escriba), 19, 64, 90
One Hundred Years of Solitude (Cien años de soledad), 3, 10, 13, 16, 19, 21, 24, 28, 29, 32, 35, 36, 39, 40, 43, 47, 50, 52, 65, 66, 83, 89, 90, 91, 94, 98, 99, 102

WORKS—SHORT FICTION
"Artificial Roses" ("Rosas artificiales"), *30–31,* 102
"Balthazar's Marvelous Afternoon" ("La prodigiosa tarde de Baltazar"), *24–27,* 90, 101
"Big Mama's Funeral" ("Los funerales de la Mamá Grande"), 6, 28, *31–35,* 66, 103, 113
"Bitterness for Three Sleepwalkers" ("Amargura para tres sonámbulos"), 8, 12, 90, 93, 96
"Blacamán, the Good, Vendor of Miracles" ("Blacamán el bueno vendedor de milagros"), *46–48,* 50, 104, 105, 106, 108, 110–11, 114, 115n6
"Death Constant beyond Love" ("Muerte constante más allá del amor"), *42–44,* 46, 50, 104, 106, 107, 109, 112, 114
"Dialogue with the Mirror" ("Diálogo del espejo"), 7, 93, 99

García Márquez, Gabriel (*Continued*)
"El invierno" (Winter), 13
"Eva Is Inside Her Cat" ("Eva
está dentro de su gato"), 5, 6,
15, 90, 91, 99
"Eyes of a Blue Dog" (Ojos de
perro azul"), 8–9, 90, 93
"Handsomest Drowned Man in
the World, The" ("El ahogado
más hermoso del mundo"), *40–
42*, 86, 104, 105, 106, 110, 114
"Incredible and Sad Tale of
Innocent Eréndira and Her
Heartless Grandmother, The"
(La increíble y triste historia de
la cándida Eréndira y de su
abuela desalmada"), *48–52*, 72,
73, 107–10, 114
"La casa" (The house), 16, 74
"Last Voyage of the Ghost Ship,
The" ("El último viaje del
buque fantasma"), *44–46*, 86,
97, 104, 105, 109, 110, 111–12
"Monologue of Isabel Watching It
Rain in Macondo" ("Monólogo
de Isabel viendo llover en
Macondo"), 13–15, 90
"Montiel's Widow" ("La viuda de
Montiel"), 24, *27–28*, 90, 101–2
"Nabo: The Black Man Who
Made the Angels Wait" ("Nabo,
el negro que hizo esperar a los
ángeles"), 11–12, 90, 95, 96–97,
99
"Night of the Curlews, The" ("La
noche de los alcaravanes"), 9–
10, 90, 93–94
"One Day after Saturday" ("Un
día después del sábado"), *28–
30*, 32, 90, 102
"One of These Days" ("Un día de
estos"), *22–23*, 100
*Rastro de tu sangre en la nieve, El;
El verano feliz de la señora Forbes*
(The trail of your blood in the
snow; Mrs. Forbes's happy
summer), 54

"Other Side of Death, The" ("La
otra costilla de la muerte"), 7,
93, 99
"Sea of Lost Time, The" ("El
mar del tiempo perdido"), *39–
40*, 43, 50, 65, 104, 105, 106,
107, 109, 114
"Someone Has Been Disarranging
These Roses" ("Alguien
desordena estas rosas"), 8–9, 15,
90
Story of a Shipwrecked Sailor, The
(*Relato de un náufrago*), 16–18
"Tubal-Caín forja una estrella"
(Tubal-Caín forges a star), 5, 6
"Tuesday Siesta" ("La siesta del
martes"), *20–22*, 28, 53, 64, 90–
91, 94, 99–100
"There Are No Thieves in This
Town" ("En este pueblo no hay
ladrones"), *23–24*, 25, 100–101
"Third Resignation, The" ("La
tercera resignación"), 5–6, 15,
90, 91–92, 99
"Very Old Man with Enormous
Wings, A" ("Un señor muy viejo
con unas alas enormes"), *37–39*,
40, 50, 104–5, 106, 109, 110,
114
"Woman Who Came at Six
O'Clock, The" ("La mujer que
llegaba a las seis"), 9, 99

General in His Labyrinth, The (*El
general en su laberinto*), 55
Gilard, Jacques, 13, 15, 16; *Textos
costeños*, 85
Goetzinger, Judith, 34, 35
Greene, Graham, 68
Grupo de Barranquilla. *See*
Barranquilla Group
Guajira Peninsula, 39, 46, 47, 48
Guibert, Rita, 63

Hancock, Joel, 50
"Handsomest Drowned Man in the
World, The" ("El ahogado más

hermoso del mundo"), *40–42*, 86, 104, 105, 106, 110, 114

Hemingway, Ernest, 9, 20, 22, 24, 26, 53, 68, 78, 97, 98

Hungary, 45

"Incredible and Sad Tale of Innocent Eréndira and Her Heartless Grandmother, The" ("La increíble y triste historia de la cándida Eréndira y de su abuela desalmada"), *48–52*, 72, 73, 107–10, 114

In Evil Hour (*La mala hora*), 19, 22, 24, 28, 30, 94, 98, 100–101

James, Henry, 97

Janes, Regina, 36, 45, 47, 52, 83

journalism, *15–16*, 65, 72, 79, 83, *84–89*

Joyce, James, 42, 78

Kafka, Franz, 68, 85; *Metamorphosis, The*, 5, 6, 7, 65, 77, 86–87, 91

"La casa" (The house), 16

"La Sierpe" series, 16

la violencia (Colombian civil wars), 4, 27, 58n25, 97

Lam, Wilfredo, 70

"Last Voyage of the Ghost Ship" ("El último viaje del buque fantasma"), *44–46*, 86, 97, 104, 105, 109, 110, 111–12

Lazarillo de Tormes, 67

Leaf Storm (*La hojarasca*), 6, 10, 12, 13, 16, 19, 20, 28, 29, 64, 74, 90, 91, 94, 96, 97, 98

Liberal party, 4

Linker, Susan Mott, 24–25

Love in the Time of Cholera (*El amor en los tiempos del cólera*), 3, 44, 54, 55

McGrady, Donald, 12, 16

McMurray, George R., 24, 47, 50

McNerney, Kathleen, 22, 51, 83

Macondo, 13, 19, 28, 29, 53, 68, 74, 86

Magdalena River, 4

magical realism, 9, 34, 35, 36, 66

"Marquesa" fiction, 16

Marx, Karl, 80

Mendoza, Plinio Apuleyo, 3, 10, 20, 63

Miller, Beth, 26

Millington, Mark, 37, 45, 47, 83

Minotaur, myth of, 50

"Monologue of Isabel Watching It Rain in Macondo" ("Monólogo de Isabel viendo llover en Macondo"), 13–15, 90

"Montiel's Widow" ("La viuda de Montiel"), 24, *27–28*, 90, 101–2

Mutis, Alvaro, 16

"Nabo: The Black Man Who Made the Angels Wait" ("Nabo, el negro que hizo esperar a los ángeles"), 11–12, 90, 95, 96–97, 99

name symbolism, 26

Neruda, Pablo, 69

"Night of the Curlews, The" ("La noche de los alcaravanes"), 9–10, 90, 93–94

No One Writes to the Colonel (*El coronel no tiene quien le escriba*), 19, 64, 90

Nobel Prize in literature, 3, 55, 78, 83, 85

novel of social protest, 71

Núñez de Arce, Gaspar, 68

"One Day after Saturday" ("Un día después del sábado"), *28–30*, 32, 90, 102

One Hundred Years of Solitude (*Cien años de soledad*), 3, 10, 13, 16, 19, 21, 24, 28, 29, 32, 35, 36, 39, 40, 43, 47, 50, 52, 65, 66, 83, 89, 90, 91, 94, 98, 99, 102

"One of These Days" ("Un día de estos"), *22–23*, 100

"Other Side of Death, The" ("La otra costilla de la muerte), 7, 93, 99

Palencia-Roth, Michael, 52
Peel, Roger M., 33
Penuel, Arnold M., 49, 50
Piedra y Cielo (Stone and Sky poets), 4
Pierce, Robert N., 15
Pigafetta, Antonio: *First Voyage Around the World*, 67

Quevedo, Francisco de, 42–43, 59n38, 115n5

Rastro de tu sangre en la nieve, El; El verano feliz de la señora Forbes (The trail of your blood in the snow; Mrs. Forbes's happy summer), 54
Redford, Robert, 55
Rimbaud, Arthur, 68, 69
Rojas Pinilla, Gustavo, 17

Sacerio-Garí, Enrique, 31
Saint-Exupéry, Antoine de, 67
St. Stephen, 42
Sartre, Jean-Paul, 79
Schumann, William Howard, 68
"Sea of Lost Time, The" ("El mar del tiempo perdido"), *39–40*, 44, 50, 65, 104, 105, 106, 107, 109, 114
Simon, Marlise, 63
Sims, Robert L., 8, 35
solitude, 76, 91, 92
"Someone Has Been Disarranging These Roses" ("Alguien desordena estas rosas"), 8–9, 15, 90
Sophocles, 68; *Oedipus Rex*, 67, 77
Story of a Shipwrecked Sailor, The (*Relato de un náufrago*), 16–18

Sucre (Sincelejo), 10, 19
Sundance Institute, 55

"There Are No Thieves in This Town" ("En este pueblo no hay ladrones"), *23–24*, 25, 100–101
Theseus, 50
"Third Resignation, The" ("La tercera resignación"), 5–6, 15, 90, 91–92, 99
Tolstoy, Leo: *War and Peace*, 67
Treaty of Neerlandia, 98
"Tubal-Caín forja una estrella" (Tubal-Caín forges a star), 7
"Tuesday Siesta" ("La siesta del martes"), *20–22*, 28, 53, 64, 90–91, 94, 99–100

United Fruit Company, 77
Up de Graff, F. W., 66

Valéry, Paul, 69
vallenatos (popular coastal songs), 69, 71n1
Vargas Llosa, Mario, 3, 6, 8, 9, 76, 90, 91
Velasco, Luis Alejandro, 17–18
"Very Old Man with Enormous Wings, A" ("Un señor muy viejo con unas alas enormes"), *37–39*, 40, 59, 104–5, 106, 109, 110, 114
Vinyes, Ramón, 10

Williams, Raymond L., 7, 14, 15, 16, 24, 33–34, 40, 50–51, 83
"Woman Who Came at Six O'Clock, The" (La mujer que llegaba a las seis"), 9, 99
Woolf, Virginia, 53; *Mrs. Dalloway*, 67–68, 98

Yoknapatawpha County, 4

Zipaquirá, 4, 68

The Author

Harley D. Oberhelman is a graduate of the University of Kansas, where he received the B.S., M.A., and Ph.D. degrees. He has been a professor at Texas Tech University since 1958. His principal area of interest is Spanish American contemporary literature. He held a Fulbright teaching award at the National University of Tucumán in Argentina and has received research grants for study in South America, including two in Colombia for research on García Márquez. Oberhelman is the author of the 1970 Twayne volume *Ernesto Sábato* and *The Presence of Faulkner in the Writings of García Márquez* (1980). He has published some 40 critical studies and 2 textbooks.

The Editor

Gordon Weaver earned his Ph.D. in English and creative writing at the University of Denver, and is currently professor of English at Oklahoma State University. He is the author of several novels, including *Count a Lonely Cadence*, *Give Him a Stone*, *Circling Byzantium*, and most recently *The Eight Corners of the World*. His short stories are collected in *The Entombed Man of Thule*, *Such Waltzing Was Not Easy*, *Getting Serious*, *Morality Play*, and *A World Quite Round*. Recognition of his fiction includes the St. Lawrence Award for Fiction (1973), two National Endowment for the Arts fellowships (1974 and 1989), and the O. Henry First Prize (1979). He edited *The American Short Story, 1945–1980: A Critical History* and is currently editor of the *Cimarron Review*. Married and the father of three daughters, he lives in Stillwater, Oklahoma.